POSTWAR LITERATURE: 1945 TO THE PRESENT

English literature in its historical, cultural and social contexts

Caroline Merz
Patrick Lee-Browne

Evans Brothers Limited

Published by
Evans Brothers Limited
2A Portman Mansions
Chiltern Street
London W1U 6NR

© Evans Brothers Limited 2003

First published in 2003

Printed in Hong Kong by Wing King Tong Co. Ltd

British Library Cataloguing in Publication Data

Merz, Caroline
    Post-war literature: 1945 to the present. –
    (Backgrounds to English literature)
    1. English literature – 20th century – History
    and Criticism
    2. Great Britain – Intellectual life – 1945 –
    I.Title
    820.9'00914

    ISBN 0237522586

Editor: Jinny Johnson
Consultant: Peter Childs
Design: Simon Borrough
Production: Jenny Mulvanny

Acknowledgements

Cover: the art archive/Mr and Mrs Clark and
              Percy 1970-71, © David Hockney
Title page: Corbis
p.7:   Topham Picturepoint
p.11:   Ronald Grant Archive
p.15:   Hulton Getty
p.17:   (top) Houston Rogers/Theatre
              Museum, V&A (bottom) Corbis
p.35:   Topham Picturepoint
p.37:   (top) the art archive
              (bottom) Topham Picturepoint
p.43:   Topham Picturepoint
p.47:   Topham Picturepoint
p.55:   Topham Picturepoint
p.65   The Bridgeman Art Library
p.73:   Topham Picturepoint
p.79:   Topham Picturepoint

**For permission to use copyright material, the
author and publisher gratefully acknowledge the
following:**

p.36: From *The New Poetry* by Al Alvarez (Penguin
Books, 1962). UK & Commonwealth rights by permis-
sion of Penguin (UK) Ltd. US rights by permission of
Gillon Aitken Associates Ltd.

p.16, 18: From *Waiting For Godot* by Samuel Beckett.
By permission of Faber and Faber Ltd.

p.10: 'St Saviour's, Aberdeen Park, Highbury, London
N.' from *Collected Poems* by John Betjeman. By permission of John Murray (Publishers) Ltd.

p.57: From *Serious Money* by Caryl Churchill. By permission of Methuen Publishing Ltd.

p.70-71: From 'Standing Female Nude' and 'Mean
Time' by Carol Ann Duffy, published by Anvil Press
Poetry in 1985 and 1993. By permission of Anvil
Press Poetry Ltd.

p.49: From *Translations* by Brian Friel. UK &
Commonwealth rights by permission of Faber and
Faber Ltd. US rights by permission of The Catholic
University of America Press.

p.62: From 'v' by Tony Harrison, 1985. By permission
of Bloodaxe Books.

p.38: From 'Afternoons' and 'Annus Mirabilis' from
Collected Poems by Philip Larkin. By permission of
Faber and Faber Ltd.

p.60: From *The Child in Time* by Ian McEwan, pub-
lished by Jonathan Cape. Reprinted by permission of
The Random House Group Ltd throughout the UK and
Commonwealth. US rights by permission of Rogers,
Coleridge & White Ltd, 20 Powis Mews, London W11
1JN.

p.9: From *Love in a Cold Climate* by Nancy Mitford
(Copyright © Nancy Mitford, 1949) by permission of
PFD on behalf of the estate of Nancy Mitford.

p.32: From *Loot* by Joe Orton. UK & Commonwealth
rights by permission of Methuen Publishing Ltd. US
rights by permission of Grove Press.

p.20: From *Look Back in Anger* by John Osbourne. UK
& Commonwealth rights by permission of Faber and
Faber Ltd. US rights by permission of Helen Osbourne.

p.61: From 'A Martian Sends a Postcard Home' by
Craig Raine. By permission of David Godwin
Associates.

p.19: From *Under Milk Wood* by Dylan Thomas, copyright © 1952 by Dylan Thomas. UK & Commonwealth
rights by permission of David Higham Associates Ltd.
US rights by permission of New Directions Publishing
Corp.

Every effort has been made to trace the copyright
holders, but in some cases this has not proved possible. The publisher will be happy to rectify any such
errors in future reprints and/or new editions.

CONTENTS

1. THE YEARS OF AUSTERITY

'In a very real sense these austerity years were a threshold to the whole first post-war era: rock-hard and grey, whitened maybe by dedication and labour, but opening on the warmer times within' (Arthur Marwick, *British Society Since 1945*).

In 1945, Britain had won a war. But after the initial triumph and celebrations of VE Day there was little to make people feel they were part of a victorious nation. Britain was impoverished by six long years of bombing and deprivation. The British Empire still existed, but it was steadily diminishing, while the 'super-powers', America and Russia, were now dominant. Despite this, there was a mood of stoicism, even optimism, which carried people through the years of austerity that followed.

The Welfare State

The Labour Party came to power under the leadership of prime minister Clement Attlee in the general election of July 1945, with its first overall majority. The overwhelming defeat of the war hero Winston Churchill – leader of the Conservative Party – was in some ways surprising, but it was the natural outcome of the experience of the war and of the aspirations created by its ending. The new government continued with the process, begun during wartime, of creating a Welfare State in which central government, together with local authorities, took on responsibility for creating security for all its citizens, rich or poor, 'from the cradle to the grave'. The best remembered achievements of this reforming Labour government include the founding of the National Health Service in 1946 and the National Insurance Act passed in the same year. The government nationalised many industries, including coal in 1946, electricity in 1947 and the railways in 1948.

In spite of the reforming enthusiasm of Attlee's cabinet, however, this was still an era of austerity, as the long-term economic impact of the war became clear. British people had few, if any, of the luxuries enjoyed by their American counterparts. In the immediate post-war years almost everything was rationed, including basic foodstuffs such as flour and eggs, as well as clothing, petrol, chocolates and sweets, and other essential items like soap. Between July 1946 and July 1948 even bread was rationed. A series of economic crises, including the drastic devaluation of the pound against the dollar in 1949, highlighted Britain's economic decline and its new relationship of dependence on the USA.

In the years after 1945, leading figures of all political parties came to agree on certain assumptions about the development of British society. The radicalism of the Labour government was limited; it offered no challenge to key institutions such as the public schools and the monarchy, which remained off-limits for reform. For its part, the Conservative opposition soon came to accept – though sometimes reluctantly – the main post-war reforms. In fact, it was a young Conservative minister in the wartime coalition, R.A. Butler, who had shaped the new Education Act in 1944, making secondary education available to all children. These consensus values underlying political debates were crucial to the British post-war experience, and it was not till the advent of Margaret Thatcher in 1979 that their dominance would be seriously challenged.

Our American friends

Britain emerged from World War II deeply in debt to the Americans. Many cities such as London and Coventry had been devastated by repeated aerial attacks. Rebuilding these cities would take many years and a great deal of money. Government housing policy was to get rid of slums and build new council housing estates, often on the edges of towns. Funding for rebuilding and for the government's wider programme of social reforms had to come from somewhere, and much of it was borrowed from the USA.

Although Anglo-American research had produced atomic bombs which devastated Nagasaki and Hiroshima, the US McMahon Act of 1946 prevented Britain from taking any further part in the research. However, the foreign secretary, Ernest Bevin, resolved that Britain would build its own bomb, correctly perceiving that nuclear capability would secure Britain a place 'at the top table' in international affairs. This bomb was first tested in Australia on 3 October 1952.

The Iron Curtain

America and Britain continued to work together. But Britain's relationship with its other major wartime ally, the Soviet Union, was entirely different. In 1946 the former prime minister Winston Churchill made a speech in the USA in which he proclaimed 'From Stettin in the Baltic to Trieste in the Adriatic, an iron curtain has descended across the Continent'. He was warning that the differences between the Western, capitalist world and the Eastern, communist world now seemed irreconcilable, and that the Soviet Union under Stalin's leadership was seeking 'indefinite expansion' of its 'powers and doctrines'. The Cold War, as this political tension between East and West became known, began with American anxiety about the Soviets' plans for expansion. Cold War paranoia quickly spread to Britain, where dissenters were sometimes branded Soviet supporters or communists. The Civil Service was purged of 'communists' in 1948 and the John Lewis Partnership ordered, in April 1949, the dismissal of any employee in its department stores who refused to sign an anti-communist declaration.

Women: back to the kitchen sink?

One of the main problems facing the government in 1945 was unemployment. As had been the case after World War I, men returning from the war needed work. In order to find jobs for them, married women, who had been persuaded to do their bit for the war effort by working in factories and on the land, were now encouraged to relinquish their role as paid workers and take up the more 'feminine' roles of housewife and mother once again. Many women left their jobs immediately after the war, but others were reluctant to give up their new-found independence. Women's new post-war role became the subject of intense public argument, and the dominant feature of many women's lives was anxiety and uncertainty about their future.

The immediate post-war years were a drab and dreary let-down for women in other ways. Britain had been promised peace and plenty: but when peace did come, expectations of 'plenty' were quickly shattered. It was the woman of the household who was expected to work out ways of coping with inadequate rations of essential items and food shortages. At the same time, the marriage rate was higher than ever and there was a post-war 'baby boom', just as there had been after World War I. For married women and mothers who did return to work (as they were encouraged to, briefly, in 1947) there were no social facilities such as nurseries or late shopping hours. But from 1948 onwards, with the introduction of the NHS and a social security scheme, alongside the government's programme of house building and repairs, women began to see an improvement in their daily lives.

The 'New Look'

Alongside practical tips on ways for women to 'make do and mend', women's magazines were – then as now – full of fashion and beauty features. Certainly, the war and then rationing had made glamour and looking good difficult to achieve. In 1947 the Parisian fashion

—GEORGE ORWELL—

Two of the most famous novels of the period, Animal Farm *(1945) and* Nineteen Eighty-four *(1949), are concerned with movements in global politics. Both were the work of the writer George Orwell (the pseudonym of Eric Blair, 1903-50), a consistent critic of the way in which political idealism easily declines into bureaucracy and totalitarianism.* Animal Farm *satirises this process in the form of a fable in which Stalinist pigs establish a farmyard dictatorship, enjoying the fruits of the other animals' hard work and making deals with the very men against whom they have sworn enmity. Written during the war, it was denied publication for obvious reasons until 1945, and was followed in 1949 by* Nineteen Eighty-Four. *This is a more grimly realistic vision of life in a totalitarian state, in which independent thought itself becomes a crime and the population is conditioned through fear to believe everything the propaganda machine creates.*

The novel's enduring hold on the imagination is evidenced by the way it has provided the concepts for two television series 50 years later: Big Brother *(who in the novel is ceaselessly 'Watching You' via the ubiquitous telescreens), and* Room 101, *named after the room where the everyman hero Winston Smith's oppressors finally break his spirit by confronting him with what he fears most. In* Nineteen Eighty-Four, *Fascism and Communism seem to merge into a single totalitarian force. The world is permanently at war, the war being used to justify privation and to rally the masses. Ironically, Orwell based his 'Ministry of Truth', in which Winston works, largely on the BBC, where he had worked as part of the wartime propaganda machine.*

Christian Dior's 'New Look'
A model wears clothes from Dior's New Look
collection of 1947. A feature of the collection
was the amount of fabric used in the clothes – as
seen in this skirt – in reaction to the rationing and
austerity of the war years.

designer Christian Dior decided that women had spent long enough wearing dungarees and practical work clothes, and created a collection of clothes so extravagant and controversial that it was initially greeted with outrage. The 'New Look', as the collection was called, involved skirts with anything up to 25 metres of fabric. Dior thought women wanted elegance and glamour, and he was proved right. Although it may have seemed frivolous, the New Look addressed the need for fantasy, as well as food and provisions, in the years of austerity. It is possible to see the New Look as an example of cultural renewal similar to that taking place in other areas of society, but it can also be seen as an example of a backward-looking tendency, with the extravagant but impractical clothes signalling a return to an old-fashioned idea of femininity.

Class and culture: the Arts Council and the BBC

World War II had, of necessity and in some cases only temporarily, broken down some of the class barriers in Britain. The skills and experience of people from all walks of life were needed for the war effort, and for a short time it seemed as if this new spirit might continue into peacetime. But Britain was still a class-based society, and the divisions which had existed since the beginning of the 20th century remained, although there was more social mobility than in the pre-war years.

During wartime, members of the public had been hungry for culture, which helped them both to escape from and to make sense of what they were experiencing. It was hard for publishers affected by paper shortages to keep up with the demand for reading matter of all kinds, ranging from popular novels to reprints of the classics and journals such as *Picture Post*. Classical music, Shakespearean drama and documentary films reached unusually wide and appreciative audiences. This kind of inclusive 'national' culture continued to be promoted after the war both by the BBC and by the Arts Council, formed in 1946 from the wartime Council for the Encouragement of Music and the Arts (CEMA).

For the first time, central government was taking on some responsibility for funding the arts in Britain. The Arts Council became an important channel of government subsidy towards music and the other arts, although the audience it served was mainly an elite one, similar to the highbrow audience targeted by the BBC's Third Programme, launched in 1946. Civic (local authority) sponsorship also played an important part in reaffirming the importance of the arts after the destruction of so many theatres, concert halls and art galleries during the Blitz. The most significant civic venture was the launching in 1947 of the Edinburgh International Festival of Music and Drama, which by its nature was a testimonial to the new, post-war spirit of international reconciliation and understanding.

BBC radio, which had no competition from commercial radio, had played an enormous part in keeping people informed, educated and entertained during the war, as well as helping to keep up morale. It emerged from the war with a much enhanced reputation, and for a few years BBC radio broadcasting experienced a brief flowering. The wartime Forces and Home programmes continued under the new titles of the Light Programme and the Home Service, but in 1946 a major new development took place. The Third Programme, as it was called, was aimed at a 'perceptive and intelligent' audience, and devoted entirely to classical music, drama and literature. Literature played a big part in the Third Programme's output, and some of the most prominent contemporary writers, including T.S. Eliot (1888-1965), Elizabeth Bowen (1899-1973), George Orwell and Louis MacNeice (1907-63), broadcast regularly.

Writers looking backwards: Waugh, Mitford and Betjeman

Some of the most popular and critically acclaimed writers of the immediate post-war years were those who looked back to the pre-war years in their works.

Nancy Mitford (1904-73) came from a highly eccentric aristocratic family. She was one of the four daughters of Lord Redesdale; one sister became a communist, another married the British fascist leader Oswald Mosley and a third sister was an ardent admirer of Hitler. Nancy published three novels before her first popular success, *The Pursuit of Love* (1945) which was followed by *Love in a Cold Climate* (1949). In both these comic novels she draws on her own experience to capture the speech, manner and codes of the upper class with stinging accuracy: 'I have seen too many children brought up without Nannies to think this at all desirable.' Mitford's reckless and often bohemian characters are determined to find life 'amusing' at all costs. These novels are also consciously backward-looking: Mitford is writing about a social order that, to a great extent, is already history. Perhaps this is why her novels became so popular with women readers looking for escapism in the post-war years: Mitford is unconcerned with the public crises going on around her, and the war casts no shadow over either book.

Another deliberately backward-looking writer is Evelyn Waugh (1903-66), whose literary career had already prospered in the 1930s with comic and satirical novels such as *Vile Bodies* (1930), *Black Mischief* (1932), and *A Handful of Dust* (1934). One of Waugh's most popular works is *Brideshead Revisited*, published in 1945, which struck a more serious note than his previous books. The novel opens during World War II, in circumstances which lead the main character, Charles Ryder, to recall nostalgically the frail securities of a bygone age, through sumptuous descriptions of the luxury of English country-house life. To Waugh, the social upheaval caused by war – including the recognition of the role of women, the loosening of the class structure, increased opportunities and the influence of American culture and politics on British life – was regrettable. He thought it would lead to mediocrity and the lowering of cultural standards in general. Waugh's *Sword of Honour* trilogy (*Men at Arms*, 1952; *Officers and Gentlemen*, 1955; *Unconditional Surrender*, 1961) involves more nostalgia, this time for the shared experience of military life, coupled with a bitter awareness of the failures of war.

Poets didn't usually achieve the popularity of successful novelists and playwrights, but John Betjeman (1906-87) was the exception. His blend of nostalgia and quirky, very English humour held enormous appeal for middle-class readers, and the publication of his *Selected Poems* (1948) turned him into a best-selling poet. Like Waugh, Betjeman laments in his work what he sees as the gradual and secretive spread of cultural decline and mediocrity, but there is always a sense of affection for other people that is sometimes absent in Waugh's satire.

Leisure time

Whatever walk of life people came from, material conditions in the post-war years were different from those before the war. Despite the problems brought about by rationing and shortages, surveys showed that the nation as a whole was healthier and fitter in 1951 than it had ever been before. From 1948 onwards almost all Britain's schoolchildren were given free milk to drink at school. Children in all sections of the community were taller and heavier than in 1936, and the infant mortality rate also dropped significantly. BBC Television, which had begun in 1936 – but closed down for the duration of the war – started up again in 1946, although few homes owned a TV set until the early 1950s. For the time being, radio was still the dominant medium for entertainment at home.

— BETJEMAN'S LONDON —

Betjeman's nostalgia for the London changed forever by the physical and social effects of the war is evident in 'St. Saviour's, Aberdeen Park, Highbury, London, N.'

> *With oh such peculiar branching and over-reaching*
> *   of wire*
> *Trolley-bus standards pick their threads from the*
> *   London sky*
> *Diminishing up the perspective, Highbury-bound*
> *   retire*
> *Threads and buses and standards with plane-trees*
> *   volleying by*
> *And, more peculiar still, that ever-increasing spire*
> *Bulges over the housetops, polychromatic and high.*
>
> *Stop the trolley-bus, stop! And here, where the roads*
> *   unite*
> *Of weariest worn-out London – no cigarettes, no*
> *   beer,*
> *No repairs undertaken, nothing in stock – alight;*
> *For over the waste of willow-herb, look at her, sailing*
> *   clear,*
> *A great Victorian church, tall, unbroken and bright*
> *In a sun that's setting in Willesden and saturating*
> *   us here.*

Evelyn Waugh's *Brideshead Revisited* (1945)
Adapted for television in 1981

The Granada TV series of *Brideshead Revisited* attracted huge audiences
in Britain and the United States. It was an early example of the modern
'heritage' genre in television and cinema, which exploits English
landscape, architecture and culture in a nostalgic spirit.

Cinema: literary connections

Possibly the most significant medium for focusing the mood and aspirations of the post-war years was the cinema. British cinema had an uneven history but was generally seen as having enjoyed its 'golden age' during the war, and the impetus was continued into the post-war years. In 1946 each member of the population went to the cinema on average 30 times a year, ten times more often than in the year 2000.

Both critics and audiences found themselves, for a short period, rating British films as highly as Hollywood ones. There were successful adaptations of literary classics such as *Great Expectations* (filmed by David Lean in 1946), *Oliver Twist* (Lean, 1948), and *Hamlet* (Laurence Olivier, 1948). Many leading playwrights and novelists, including Terence Rattigan (1911-77), J.B. Priestley (1894-1984) and Eric Ambler (1909-98), wrote directly for the screen, either adapting their own works or creating new ones; the best example is Graham Greene (1904-91), whose crime novel *Brighton Rock* (co-scripted by Rattigan) was filmed by John Boulting in 1947, and whose original story *The Third Man*, set in Vienna and directed by Carol Reed in 1949, became a huge international success.

The cinema also developed some expert writers of its own, encouraging them to write imaginatively for the screen in ways which owed nothing to literary or theatrical models. T.E.B. Clarke helped to create the distinctive public image of Ealing Studios with his scripts for the whimsical comedy *Passport to Pimlico* (1949) and the police drama *The Blue Lamp* (1949), while writer Emeric Pressburger and director Michael Powell produced some of the most memorable works of the period, including *I Know Where I'm Going* (1945), *A Matter of Life and Death* (1946) and *The Red Shoes* (1948).

Theatre after 1945

As with the post-war novel, traditional forms and themes continued to dominate. It was to be several years before new voices would be

—MERVYN PEAKE AND—
GORMENGHAST

It isn't always easy to trace works of art and literature to a particular social or historic background. One example is the Gormenghast *trilogy by Mervyn Peake (1911-68), consisting of* Titus Groan *(1946),* Gormenghast *(1950) and* Titus Alone *(1959). Peake had worked as a war artist in World War II, recording among other things the scenes of human suffering that confronted the Allies when they moved into Belsen concentration camp in 1945. His three novels are Gothic fantasies, recounting the life of Titus, 77th Earl of Groan, in his crumbling castle of Gormenghast.*

Titus is surrounded by a weird cast of characters including Dr Prunesquallor and the melancholy Muzzlehatch. Unlike Orwell's Animal Farm *(see page 6), which can clearly be read as an allegory of contemporary events, the extraordinary and grotesque world of Gormenghast appears to have little direct relationship with the politics or culture of post-war Europe. Gormenghast, like Tolkien's Middle Earth (see page 24) is a self-contained fantastical world. But the trilogy's themes of a decaying civilisation and an antiquated hierarchical system – which lies like a dead weight on Titus – can be read as an expression of the need for social change, in particular the rebellion of the young against the old. Peake has been hailed as one of the great literary and artistic geniuses of the 20th century. He illustrated most of his own work, as well as illustrating books by other authors and writing poetry, including* The Glassblowers *(1950).*

heard and alternative modes of production employed. For the time being, however, 'serious' theatrical productions were dominated by the works of writers who had come to prominence in the 1930s, such as J.B. Priestley, Somerset Maugham (1874-1965), Noel Coward (1899-1973) and Terence Rattigan – as well as the classics, which almost always meant Shakespeare.

Terence Rattigan's *The Winslow Boy* (1946) is based on a real lawsuit from 1908, and in the play Rattigan dramatises the conflict between individual liberty and the interests of the Establishment. It concerns the efforts of an apparently old-fashioned, reactionary barrister to clear the name of a young naval cadet wrongly accused of stealing a postal order. In the confrontation between the 'small man' and the Establishment, the ultimate victory of the small man is a sign of the breaking down of old social controls, and the optimistic stirring of a new, fairer society. Rattigan's other plays focus on failed relationships and sexual repression. *The Browning Version* (1948), about a struggling, inadequate schoolmaster at a minor public school with an unfaithful wife, is characteristic of such dramas. Rattigan's plays were considered to be perfect examples of the 'well-made play' (see Glossary of Terms), and continue to be popular with audiences to this day.

J.B. Priestley's *An Inspector Calls* (1945) is another enduringly popular play which captured the mood of optimism at the end of war and the desire to create some new form of social order. Like Rattigan's *The Winslow Boy*, Priestley's play has a historical setting (1912) but the audience is clearly invited to make comparisons with contemporary society. Priestley is suggesting that the problems he raises – chiefly associated with class and privilege – remain unsolved. The police inspector of the title is a 'deus ex machina' figure who comes from nowhere to detect and expose moral corruption and guilt in the privileged world that is the setting of the play, represented by the members of a wealthy industrialist's family. The message of *An Inspector Calls* is that 'progress' has less to do with technical developments than an acceptance of moral responsibility for others and of the need for political change.

—VERSE DRAMA—

In 1946 the Mercury Theatre in London launched a programme of new plays written in verse, and for a few years verse drama enjoyed a brief revival as an 'advanced' alternative to the conventionally constructed plays of writers such as Priestley and Rattigan. The poets W.H. Auden and Christopher Isherwood (1904-86) had collaborated on several politically motivated verse plays before the war, such as The Ascent of F6 *(1936). The best-known exponents of post-war verse drama were T.S. Eliot (1888-1966) and Christopher Fry (1907-). Eliot had already had some success with plays written in verse in the 1930s, particularly* Murder in the Cathedral *(1935), but in these post-war years the main impetus for the revival came from a desire to present some of the richness of Britain's historical, artistic and Christian heritage in a form which broke with convention in order to express the modern age. Most of the new plays were set in the past, had religious themes, and drew on the conventions of Elizabethan drama and the 17th-century masque. Christopher Fry's* The Lady's Not for Burning *(1948) was set in the late Middle Ages, starred John Gielgud, and had a long West End run – but in the end the vogue for verse drama proved short-lived, and ended in the early 1950s as suddenly as it had begun.*

2. THE 1950S: FROM AUSTERITY TO BOOM

In the 1950s a new era was beginning, and by the middle of the decade the 'post-war' era could truly be said to be over. This was partly because the economic controls and restrictions, such as rationing, that followed the war had now been loosened or broken. In July 1954 the government announced the end of all rationing after 14 years, and ration books were burned in celebration. New processes and controls in industry and entertainment were altering the pattern of life, but the main reason for the change in atmosphere was that a new generation was emerging which had only known life since the end of the war.

The Conservative Party was returned to power with a small majority in the general election of 1951. The post-war Labour government had attempted to make Britain a more equal society through high taxation, controls of various sorts and the development of social services on an unprecedented scale, but now there was a public reaction against rationing and controls, and what some people saw as Labour's misguided attempts to impose equality. The Conservatives remained in office for 13 years, increasing their majority in 1955 when Anthony Eden became prime minister on Churchill's retirement. In 1957, Harold Macmillan replaced Eden following the Suez Crisis (see page 24). 'Supermac', as he was subsequently named, went on to win the election of 1959, and was briefly succeeded by Alec Douglas-Home in 1963.

On the whole, the mainstream of the Conservative Party felt it had to accommodate the changes which took place under Labour. It was largely because of a change in worldwide trading practices that living standards began to go up in the 1950s; controls were fully relaxed, rationing abolished and open encouragement given to private enterprise. But on the whole the spirit of 'consensus' prevailed in Britain, with a shared understanding between different social classes that money needed to be spent both on welfare services and on the arts. It was an unchallenged assumption that Britain led the world with its Welfare State.

A tonic to the nation

On 4 May 1951 the Festival of Britain on London's South Bank was opened by King George VI. One of the main purposes of the exhibition, a fantasy world created on 11 hectares of cleared bombsites, was to help dispel the gloom caused by the continuing post-war austerities. The Festival's director, Sir Gerald Barry, called it 'a tonic to the nation'. It set out to display to the world the 'best

The Skylon,
Festival of Britain
1951

The Skylon was one of the architectural features of the Festival of Britain, on London's South Bank. A temporary construction, it was an aluminium tower that gave the impression from a distance of being unsupported. Contemporary accounts noted that it resembled a huge exclamation mark.

of British' in all aspects of culture, but particularly in art and design. Britain wanted to show that it was still an international cultural leader, despite its economic dependence on the United States. The image the Festival wanted to create was of a nation securely built upon centuries of cultural tradition, but also a nation that was forward looking and innovative, demonstrated through modern design and a display of Britain's recent scientific and technological achievement. The Festival of Britain remains significant today because of its effect on modern architecture: the merits of the South Bank buildings, including the Festival Hall, are still argued over. It represented a turning point in helping to modernise public tastes in art, architecture, and particularly interior design.

Literature and drama in the 1950s

By the early 1950s a new generation of British novelists, playwrights and poets had started to make an explicit stand against what they saw as outdated modes of writing belonging to a pre-war society that no longer existed. They were reacting against the cosy world of English literature and drama as it stood, and set out to write with a new voice. The content was innovatory; sometimes the form was too.

Probably the most important event in the development of British drama in the late 1950s was the presentation at the Royal Court (see page 18) of *Waiting for Godot* by the Irishman Samuel Beckett (1906-89). Beckett wrote in French, and the play had been first staged in Paris in 1953. *Waiting for Godot* takes the art of inaction to its logical and extreme conclusion. The two tramps Vladimir and Estragon spend the play discussing the imminent arrival of Godot, but Godot never materialises, and nothing happens in the course of the 'action' of the play. The play belongs in the tradition of the 'Theatre of the Absurd' (see Glossary of Terms), in that it is both pessimistic and subversively comic.

VLADIMIR: You must be happy, too, deep down, if you only knew it.

— THE CORONATION —

The mood of celebration in 1951 quickly turned to a widespread sense of shock and loss when King George VI died unexpectedly in February 1952. He was succeeded by his elder daughter, Elizabeth (then aged only 27) and the coronation of the new Queen was awaited by the British public with enthusiasm. Surveys showed that the coronation was associated in many people's minds with the idea of a 'new Elizabethan age' in which, through the Commonwealth, if not through the Empire, Britain would still retain a glorious place in the world. On 2 June 1953 at least two million people turned out in the streets to watch the coronation procession, and inside Westminster Abbey were heads of state, prime ministers and other dignitaries from every corner of the globe. London witnessed its greatest celebration since the end of the war. An important new twist was that more than 20 million people (56 per cent of the adult population) watched the proceedings on television. The coronation was a turning point not just because it seemed to mark the end of austerity and the dawning of a new era, but because it also ushered in the 'television age'. Many people bought TV sets specifically to watch the coronation and shared the novel experience with neighbours and friends.

Waiting for Godot (1953) by Samuel Beckett

A still from the play's first London run in August 1955 at the Arts Theatre. Early audiences were baffled by the play's lack of action and characterisation, and two reviewers quoted lines from the play to support their opinion: 'Nothing happens, nobody comes, nobody goes, it's awful'.

Samuel Beckett (left)

Beckett was a highly influential figure in prose and dramatic writing from the 1950s until his death in 1989. Having left Ireland to settle in France before the outbreak of World War II he wrote equally in English and French.

ESTRAGON: Happy about what?

VLADIMIR: To be back with me again.

ESTRAGON: Would you say so?

VLADIMIR: Say you are, even if it's not true.

ESTRAGON: What am I to say?

VLADIMIR: Say, I am happy.

ESTRAGON: I am happy.

VLADIMIR: So am I.

ESTRAGON: So am I.

VLADIMIR: We are happy.

ESTRAGON: We are happy. (*Silence.*) What do we do, now that we're happy?

VLADIMIR: Wait for Godot. (*Estragon groans. Silence.*) Things have changed since yesterday.

ESTRAGON: And it he doesn't come?

VLADIMIR: (*After a moment's incomprehension*) We'll see when the time comes.

Many of the audience walked out in disgust at the first performance, so great was the shock and incomprehension of this strange play in which 'nothing happens, nobody comes, nobody goes', and in which there is only a single tree for a set. It was only later that the complexity and humour of Beckett's work came to be more widely appreciated.

Protest writers

In the early 1950s a mood of anxiety prevailed among many artists and writers that Britain was facing cultural decay as a result both of the loss of its Empire, and of the ever-growing influence of American culture on the British way of life. The Festival of Britain (see page 14) was one way in which Britain attempted to reassert its cultural superiority. Critics and the media were keen to find an equivalent in literature, and they did so by promoting two separate (although interlinked) groups of writers who could take their place on the international scene. These came to be known as the Movement and the 'angry young men'.

— THE ROYAL COURT THEATRE—

The English Stage Company was founded in 1956 by the director George Devine (1910-66) to present modern plays and encourage new writers. Its home was, and still is, the Royal Court Theatre in London. The first production at the Royal Court was Angus Wilson's The Mulberry Bush *in April 1956. It was the Royal Court that gave a young, unknown playwright called John Osborne (1929-94) his chance with* Look Back in Anger *in 1956. Although at first this play was not particularly successful at the box office, it was supported by enthusiastic critics, particularly* The Observer *newspaper's reviewer Kenneth Tynan. Osborne's play provided the title that was soon applied to the new breed of writers: the so-called 'angry young men'.*

The English Stage Company at the Royal Court was particularly influential in promoting 'kitchen sink drama', a term applied in the late 1950s to plays by writers such as Arnold Wesker and Shelagh Delaney as well as Osborne. These plays portrayed working-class or lower-middle-class life, with an emphasis on domestic realism. They were written in part as a reaction against the drawing-room comedies and middle-class dramas of Noel Coward and Rattigan, and also helped to undermine the popularity of verse-drama productions (see page 13). The Royal Court subsequently produced many important new plays by writers including John Arden, Edward Bond, David Storey, Joe Orton, Samuel Beckett, David Hare, Brian Friel, Athol Fugard, Caryl Churchill, Howard Barker, Howard Brenton and others.

The Movement was a name coined by a literary critic, J.D. Scott, to describe a loose grouping of writers, mainly poets. including Kingsley Amis (1922-95), Donald Davie (1922-95), D.J. Enright (1920-), Thom Gunn (1929-), Elizabeth Jennings (1926-) and Philip Larkin (1922-85). Each of these writers in their different ways was reacting against various 'isms' fashionable in the 1940s, including modernism (see Glossary of Terms) and internationalism; what they appeared to represent was a kind of 'Englishness' characterised by irony, rationalism and a sense of poetic craft. Kingsley Amis, whose first volume of poems had been published in 1947, declared in 1951: 'Nobody wants any more poems about philosophers or paintings or novelists or art galleries or mythology or foreign cities or other poems. At least I hope nobody wants them.' The Movement writers, however, had little in common in terms of political attitudes or social criticism, and although their poetry was easily accessible in its traditional verse forms and conventional use of language, some critics found it to be dry and over-intellectual. By 1957 the members of the Movement had gone their different ways.

It was the second group of writers who attracted wider media attention. The original 'angry young man' was a young, unknown actor called John Osborne whose first play, *Look Back in Anger*, was presented at the Royal Court Theatre (see page 18) in May 1956, after some 25 other theatres had turned it down. The influential critic Kenneth Tynan hailed *Look Back in Anger* as 'the best young play of its decade', and its hero, Jimmy Porter, as 'the completest young pup since Hamlet'. The term 'angry young men' was quickly adopted by the media to describe other playwrights and novelists, particularly those writing 'kitchen sink drama' (see page 18), and the people they were writing about. Besides Osborne these included the playwright Arnold Wesker (1932-) and the novelists Kingsley Amis, Alan

— DYLAN THOMAS AND— UNDER MILK WOOD

To begin at the beginning: It is spring, moonless night in the small town, starless and bible-black.

The Welsh poet Dylan Thomas (1914-53) was one of the most popular and successful writers of the 1930s and '40s, but his most famous single work, Under Milk Wood, *was written shortly before his death in 1953 at the age of 39. Thomas's wild, hard-drinking behaviour made him as well known for his life as for his poems.* Under Milk Wood, *described by Thomas as a 'play for voices', went through various stages before being broadcast by the BBC in 1954, and then re-shaped again as a stage play. In the play, the listener eavesdrops on the thoughts and chatter of the inhabitants of a sleepy Welsh seaside village, Llareggub. Deeply rooted in the reality of Welsh provincial life,* Under Milk Wood *is a fantasy in which Thomas uses his characteristically artificial poetic language to summon up a world of untroubled and sleepy innocence:*

The sunny slow lulling afternoon yawns and moons through the dozy town. The sea lolls, laps and idles in, with fishes sleeping in its lap. The meadows still as Sunday, the shut-eye tasselled bulls, the goat-and-daisy dingles, nap happy and lazy.

The world of Under Milk Wood *has little to do with the real present of the 1950s, or even of the real past. Instead, Thomas is deliberately escaping the past through mythic invention. Through the medium of sound alone, his intention is to create a poem in the form of a play with a dream-like structure.*

Sillitoe (1928-), John Braine (1922-86) and John Wain (1925-94). The heroes – or anti-heroes – in 'angry young man' literature were almost invariably male working-class opportunists and sexual predators, who resented authority as a matter of course.

The action of *Look Back in Anger* takes place in a Midlands town, in the one-room flat of Jimmy Porter and his wife, Alison. Jimmy is a university graduate but earns a living from running a sweet stall. His anger is largely directed at his upper-class wife, a colonel's daughter, and against women in general:

> Slamming their doors, stamping their high heels, banging their irons and saucepans – the eternal flaming racket of the female.

Jimmy also rails against the conventions and complacencies of society represented by Alison's parents and friends. Osborne offers no alternative to the ideology underlying the society Jimmy Porter is so angry about: indeed he attacked those who looked for profound meaning in the play's most famous passage, explaining it as simply an expression of 'ordinary despair':

> There aren't any good brave causes left. If the big bang does come, and we all get killed off, it won't be in aid of the old-fashioned, grand design. It'll just be for the Brave New-nothing-very-much-thank-you. About as pointless and inglorious as stepping in front of a bus.

Among the best-known novels associated with the 'angry young man' image is John Braine's *Room at the Top* (1957). Braine, who came from a working-class background in Bradford and left his grammar school at the age of 16, had moved to London in 1950, but the setting of *Room at the Top* is one with which he was familiar: a Yorkshire town, Warley, modelled on Bradford. Joe Lampton, the narrator, is the son of a mill worker who gained an accountancy qualification while a prisoner of war in Germany. Finding himself faced by social snobbery and envying the wealth of those around him, Joe decides to beat the top people by joining them. In Warley he becomes involved both with an older woman, Alice Aisgill, who is married to a prosperous businessman, and with Susan Brown, daughter of the richest and most powerful man around. He leaves Alice to marry Susan and thus goes straight to 'the top'. Alice kills herself in a horrific car accident.

The story is told in retrospective mode: Joe is a rich man in the 1950s looking back to the early post-war years. He reflects on the way his personality has been gradually corrupted as he allows ambition to take precedence over personal affection, and sexual relationships become a means of climbing the social ladder. The novel is written in a down-to-earth and naturalistic way, showing the reduced circumstances of post-war Britain in a critical light. It is also a moral tale, in which Joe's frank reflections on himself give a psychological depth to the story of an 'angry young man'. *Room at the Top* was also converted into a popular film (1958) directed by Jack Clayton, and is now seen as a turning point in British cinema.

Lucky Jim (1954), the first novel by Kingsley Amis, was hailed by critics as *the* novel representing the 'new writing'. The hero is Jim Dixon, a lower-middle-class lecturer at a provincial university whose subversive attitudes qualified him for the title of 'angry young man'. The novel mocks what Dixon sees as the cultural pretensions of his boss, Professor Welch. *Lucky Jim* is a comic novel: in it, Amis reveals his ability to record accurately the things people actually think and indeed sometimes say, rather than what they ought to think and say in order to be polite. The idea for the novel came to Amis while visiting his friend, the poet Philip Larkin, who was at the time a librarian at Leicester University.

It was in the 1950s that writers began working across various media – playwrights writing screenplays or novelists creating scripts for television – in a way that was then unprecedented but that we now accept as normal. Thus the various genres such as 'kitchen sink' drama applied not only to theatre but also to films and television drama.

Female alternatives

Another first novel published in 1954 was *Under the Net*, the work of a young Oxford philosophy lecturer, Iris Murdoch (1919-99). Murdoch's concerns were very different from those of the 'angry young men' and her novels showed the legacy of her training as a philosopher who was well read in European literature and particularly influenced by French writers such as Jean-Paul Sartre (1905-80) and Samuel Beckett. Her output as a novelist was prolific, and in most of her books she returns time and again to the same subject matter of the balance between good and evil and between art and life. The allusive nature of her writing can be seen in a novel such as *The Black Prince* (1973), in which the figure of Hamlet lurks in the background; her best known novel is perhaps *The Sea, The Sea* (1978), which won the Booker Prize in that year.

Shelagh Delaney (1939-) was the only female writer who became well-known for 'kitchen sink' drama. Like several of her male counterparts, she came from the north of England and left school at 16, but she writes from a female perspective and her concerns are somewhat different. Delaney wrote her most successful play, *A Taste of Honey*, when she was only 17, after seeing Terence Rattigan's play *Variations on a Theme* and deciding she could do better. *A Taste of Honey*, which was first presented by

Joan Littlewood at the Theatre Royal, Stratford East in 1958, is set in a run-down boarding house in a Lancashire town. The family who live there are far removed from the conventional white, middle-class characters of playwrights such as Rattigan and Noel Coward. There is no father: only a struggling, feckless mother and her teenage daughter. The mother goes off with her seedy boyfriend, leaving her schoolgirl daughter – who is pregnant from a brief relationship with a black sailor – to create, against all the odds, an alternative family with her friend, an art student. The play sympathetically presents a series of dilemmas arising from inter-racial sexual relations, and its moral centre is represented by a young gay man. Delaney was writing years before women's liberation and gay rights organisations would begin to make their mark in the 1970s, and *A Taste of Honey* (which was adapted for the cinema in 1961 and directed by Tony Richardson) remains a remarkably progressive play.

Stevie Smith (pseudonym of Florence Margaret Smith, 1902-71) published her first volume of poetry, *A Good Time Was Had By All*, in 1937, but it was with *Not Waving But Drowning* (1957) that she really made her mark. Smith was born in Hull but brought up in north London, where she spent most of her adult life with an aunt. She is known as an 'eccentric' poet whose apparently scatty, naïve style makes her impossible to classify. Her poems are witty and enigmatic, many of them illustrated by her own comic drawings. The title poem of *Not Waving But Drowning* is perhaps the best known and most popular of her poems:

> I was much too far out all my life
> And not waving but drowning...

The rise of television

Television broadcasting by the BBC had grown only slowly in the post-war years. But as a result of the coronation of Queen Elizabeth II in 1952 (see page 16) there was a huge surge of interest in the new medium. The BBC, however, kept strict rules: TV was only broadcast for a limited number of hours every day, in order that programmes would not become an addiction or keep schoolchildren from their studies, or adults from their work. The Broadcasting Act, passed in 1954, allowed the setting up of a separate commercial television channel, and ITV was born. The arrival of commercial television in 1955 stimulated the real explosion in television ownership, and by 1960 72 per cent of the population had access to both ITV and the BBC.

Many people, including some Conservative politicians, feared that commercial television would bring a decline in the high moral and cultural standards that had been set by the BBC. Their main concern was that the introduction of advertising might lead British television towards the overt commercialism of American TV, which involved sponsorship and the advertising of products within programmes. Controls were introduced on the nature and amount of advertising that would appear on the new commercial channel and all advertisements had to be clearly separated from the programmes in 'commercial breaks'.

In the face of competition from ITV – which soon became the more popular channel – the BBC continued to see itself as having responsibility for the 'cultural enlightenment' of the listening and viewing public. The overall profile of the BBC's output was predominantly middle-class and intended to be 'culturally enriching', whereas ITV offered a range of programming targeted at audiences differentiated by class, region and age. ITV's *Coronation Street*, for example, which was first broadcast in 1960, was aimed mainly at a northern working-class audience.

In terms of serious drama it was ITV's *Armchair Theatre*, which began in 1956, that proved to be more popular and ground-breaking than the BBC alternatives. From 1958 onwards *Armchair Theatre* featured original single plays written by television playwrights such as Harold Pinter (1930-), Ted Willis (1918-92) and Alun Owen (1925-97). With plays such as Owen's *No Trams to Lime Street* (1958) and *Lena O My Lena* (1960), television made its contribution to the genre of northern, working-class realism that was taking a hold on literature, theatre and cinema in the late 1950s.

The atom bomb

Britain joined the atomic superpowers in October 1952, when scientists exploded the first British atom bomb at a site on the Monte Bello islands in northwest Australia. The bomb had been developed in secret for five years. At the same time, Britain set up its own nuclear power plants. The fledgling atomic industry suffered a serious accident in 1957, when fuel rods in one of the chimneys at the Windscale (now called Sellafield) atomic power station overheated, releasing radioactive material into the atmosphere.

The Campaign for Nuclear Disarmament (CND) was founded in 1958. In April of that year, it organised a march from London to the Atomic Weapons Research Establishment at Aldermaston as a protest against nuclear weapons. The mass protest called for Britain, Russia and the United States to stop the manufacture, testing and storage of nuclear weapons. Opinion polls showed that CND had the support of between a quarter and a third of the British public. The Cold War and fear of the bomb directly and indirectly influenced many works of art and literature during the 1950s.

While the 'kitchen sink' writers such as Sillitoe and Osborne expressed their feelings about post-war society through novels and plays with realistic, contemporary settings, characters and dialogue, the realisation that there might not be a future drove some novelists back to the past. This was not an exercise in nostalgia, but an attempt to dispose of certain myths about Britain's imperial heritage. *Lord of the Flies* (1954) by William Golding (1911-1993) is just such an example of British history being revisited in order to focus on its hidden, inglorious underside. The story concerns a group of schoolboys abandoned on a desert island who descend into savagery. Golding wrote it as an ironic contrast to the conventional boys' adventure story, exemplified by R.M. Ballantyne's Victorian story *The Coral Island*, in which some brave and ingenious boys marooned on a desert island rise to the occasion. The schoolboys in *The Lord of the Flies* soon abandon all attempts to behave like rational, civilised beings and gradually, under corrupt leadership, revert to hunting, killing and barbarous rituals. A Christ-like boy, Simon, is killed sacrificially. The 'Lord of the Flies' of the title is the god which the children come to worship as they regress towards a very primitive form of society. The two novels Golding wrote after *Lord of the Flies*, *The Inheritors* (1955) and *Pincher Martin* (1956), are also concerned with the intrinsic cruelty of man to his fellow beings.

The Cold War and the 'space race' – which began when the Soviet Union launched the world's first man-made satellite into orbit around the earth in 1957 – also had an important influence on popular literature, as well as on film and TV drama. The 1950s marked an important stage in the development of genre writing, whereby certain types of fiction – such as crime and spy fiction as well as science fiction – were no longer snobbishly rejected as being unsuitable for serious treatment. One example is John Wyndham (1903-69). Although classified as a science fiction writer, he preferred the description 'logical fantasy' for his own novels, which include *The Day of the Triffids* (1951), *The Kraken Wakes* (1953), *The Chrysalids* (1955) and *The Midwich Cuckoos* (1957). In all these novels there is a contrast between a comfortable English background and a sudden catastrophe, usually of a fantastic or monstrous kind, rather than anything technological.

The rise of youth culture

Harold Macmillan replaced Sir Anthony Eden as prime minister in 1957. Eden had resigned after the Suez crisis, in which joint British and French forces had tried and failed to seize the Suez Canal from

---

— TOLKIEN AND *THE LORD* — OF *THE RINGS*

J.R.R. Tolkien (1892-1973) is widely considered to be the father of modern fantasy fiction, and some critics have argued that The Lord of the Rings *is among the greatest works of imaginative fiction of the 20th century. Born in South Africa, Tolkien studied ancient languages at Oxford University, where he later became a professor of English language and literature. His fascination for languages led to him creating his own language and mythology in stories which contain archetypal fantasy elements of good versus evil, a fallen world and the hope of a better one, and the idea of life as a pilgrimage. Tolkien became internationally known for* The Hobbit, *published in 1937, which was an immediate popular and critical success. Its sequel, published in the mid-1950s, was the epic* The Lord of the Rings *trilogy (The Fellowship of the Ring, 1954; The Two Towers, 1954; The Return of the King, 1955). In the three books Tolkien extended the Middle Earth setting of* The Hobbit *to create a convincing and detailed imaginary world. Like Mervyn Peake's* Gormenghast *(see page 12),* The Lord of the Rings *has little if any direct relationship to the times in which it was written. But that very fact perhaps provides the key to its appeal in an increasingly homogenised and secular age.*

Egypt and topple its president, Colonel Nasser, from power. Nasser, who wanted to nationalise the canal, was promoting Arab nationalism throughout the Middle East. The Anglo-French assault upon Egypt, which began on 31 October 1956, provoked a furious response from the USA and an economic crisis threatened to follow unless Britain agreed to withdraw.

Macmillan's claim that 'You've never had it so good' (the Conservatives' unofficial campaign slogan in the 1959 general election) would herald the real explosion of mass, popular culture, but already by the mid-1950s youth culture had begun to take off. Before the '50s, there were no 'teenagers', no special fashions, music, films or reading matter to mark the period of transition between the dependency of childhood and the responsibilities of adulthood. Now, in the new Elizabethan age with its developing materialism and prosperity, young people were ready to claim a significant social and economic place in society. Most of the influences on the teenage culture that was emerging in Britain were American. The craze for rock and roll swept through Britain in 1957, after the American group Bill Haley and the Comets toured the country. Audiences jived in the aisles, just as they had done during the first rock films. Elvis Presley – well known from films such as *Loving You* (1957) – was the biggest record seller, while other popular movie stars included Marlon Brando and James Dean.

The Notting Hill race riots

A new source of social conflict in Britain in the 1950s was race. Immigration from the West Indies had started soon after the war, and racial tensions and conflicts had been present since the early 1950s. The legacy of the British Empire was a situation in which West Indians, Indians, Pakistanis and Africans were all full British subjects who were entitled to settle in Britain if they wished. Immigration was encouraged in the post-war years because of the shortage of labour, and many people came to Britain in the hope of finding work and a better standard of living. Mostly they were offered the lowest-paid, most unskilled jobs, and they congregated in the poorer areas of cities that had been hardest hit by the war. The result was overcrowding and racial tension. In September 1958 violent race rioting broke out between white youths and black immigrants in Notting Hill, West London, and there were also clashes in Nottingham.

Britain was becoming a multicultural society, but for some time this process was scarcely acknowledged in literature, other than in the novels of Colin MacInnes (1914-76): *City of Spades* (1957) and *Absolute Beginners* (1959) dealt with the new London subcultures and with the racial tensions that exploded in Notting Hill. In the cinema, racial issues were tackled in a few self-conscious 'social problem films' like *Sapphire* (1959) and *Flame in the Streets* (1961).

3. MY GENERATION: THE 'SWINGING SIXTIES'

The 1960s saw the pace of change quicken in international, social and cultural affairs to the point where many of the older generation felt that the world in which they were living was becoming barely recognisable. Advances in technology, unimaginable ten years earlier, made possible such giant leaps forward as the exploration of space and the development of heart transplant surgery. The last traces of empire disappeared in Africa as Britain, along with France and Belgium, relinquished its remaining major colonial interests. At the same time changes in the leadership of the world's superpowers seemed unable to slow the gathering momentum of the Cold War. Throughout it all, youth culture was emerging with values that seemed to contradict everything that had been assumed by the generation born between the two World Wars.

The winds of change

In 1960 the British prime minister, Harold Macmillan, angered members of the South African parliament by urging South Africa to adopt policies to promote racial equality. In a famous speech made in Cape Town, he said: 'The wind of change is blowing through this continent and, whether we like it or not, this growth of national consciousness is a political fact'. In the years that followed, country after country was to gain independence: even in South Africa and Southern Rhodesia (Zimbabwe) the continuing white hold on power was shaken under the onslaught of black unrest. In the United States the black civil rights movement, under the leadership of Martin Luther King – who was murdered by a white gunman in 1968 – fought for recognition.

A number of novels written in the 1960s illustrate different approaches to the end of formal empire. *The Raj Quartet* (1966-74) by Paul Scott (1920-78) views the same events from different characters' viewpoints in the years from 1942 up to India's independence in 1947. Scott's Booker Prize-winning *Staying On* (1977) provided a coda to the *Raj Quartet* in its portrayal of an English couple who live out their retirement in a decaying hotel after independence. A *House for Mr Biswas* (1961) by V.S. Naipaul (1932-), who was born in Trinidad of an Indian family, is a comic novel also concerned with the legacy of colonialism. Set in Trinidad, the story describes the misfortunes of Mr Biswas from birth to death, and his resilience in fighting the problems of class and race. In *Wide Sargasso Sea* (1966), the novelist Jean Rhys (1890-1979) uses Charlotte Brontë's *Jane Eyre* as the basis for her novel. In *Jane Eyre* the heroine falls in love with Mr Rochester, who is already married to Bertha Mason, an heiress from the Caribbean. Bertha suffers from a mental disorder and Rochester keeps her a prisoner in the attic of his house. Rhys sets her novel in Jamaica and focuses on the character of Bertha, renamed Antoinette Cosway. The Rochester character, who is never named, shows the true nature of imperialism, afraid of the woman of whom he has taken possession and willing to destroy a culture he makes no effort to understand. *Wide Sargasso Sea*, in which the central character is a woman who is too passionate and therefore through male eyes is deemed to be mad, is also significant for its feminist theme, prefiguring many of the novels of the 1970s.

Relations between the USA and the Soviet Union continued to deteriorate during the 1960s. The Cuban missile crisis of 1962 brought nuclear war closer than at any time before or since. The American president, John Kennedy, issued an ultimatum to First Secretary Kruschev to withdraw Soviet missiles from Cuba, where they had been stationed as a deliberate nuclear threat to the United States. The crisis that followed put the relationship between the USA and the Soviet Union under great strain, leaving permanent scars on East-West relations and helping to fuel the development of new protest groups campaigning against the proliferation of nuclear weapons. In Berlin, the newly built wall separating communist East Berlin from capitalist West Berlin stood as a powerful symbol of this confrontation. From the mid-1960s, the escalating involvement of the USA in the Vietnam war and its increasingly ugly, and futile, consequences gave rise to protests throughout the Western world.

Although in the 1960s drama provided the most direct and radical response to the changes in society, novelists also took up some of the current issues. On the threshold of the new decade, Kingsley Amis's *Take a Girl Like You* (1960) engaged wittily with the shift in the moral climate through the adventures of a demure young schoolteacher, Jenny Bunn, uncertain of how 'liberated' she wants to become under the pressure of her predatory boyfriend. A different kind of response to social change is seen in *A Clockwork Orange* (1962) by Anthony Burgess (1917-94). Set in the future, it presents a frightening Orwellian vision of an Americanised Britain in which technology is in total and nightmarish control. Its central character, Alex, is the leader of a gang of teenage delinquents who terrorise people with theft, rape, torture and murder. Regarded as mad because of his extremely violent, anti-social behaviour, Alex is captured but removed from prison, under liberal legislation, for 'Reclamation Treatment'. The treatment transforms him into an emotionally neutered being for whom art, music and sex, as well as violence, are sick-making. He has become a piece of machinery, a 'clockwork orange'. The objects of Burgess's satire are both totalitarianism (as in Orwell's *Animal Farm* and *Nineteen Eighty-*

Four; see page 6) and the liberal humanism that underlay so much thinking in the newly permissive society.

The end of the Establishment?

The Conservative government was already fragile in 1962, when Harold Macmillan sacked half his cabinet in the so-called 'night of the long knives'. The Macmillan government was further weakened in 1963 by a scandal involving sex, high society and national security which became known as the 'Profumo affair'. John Profumo, the secretary of state for war, resigned from office in June 1963 after admitting that he had lied to the House of Commons about his affair with a call-girl, Christine Keeler, whom he had met at a country house belonging to Lord Astor. Macmillan was heavily criticised for failing to deal with the affair, and he resigned in October 1963 to be replaced as prime minister by the unlikely figure of Alec Douglas-Home, who renounced his title of the 14th Earl of Home in order to sit in the House of Commons.

1964 was an important landmark in 20th-century political history because it was the year that the Labour Party returned to power after 13 years of unbroken Conservative rule. Labour's 1964 election campaign vividly expressed the contrast between the 1950s and the 1960s. The Labour leader, Harold Wilson, with his confident manner, northern accent and relative youthfulness, seemed to represent a new, classless Britain as opposed to the Establishment values personified by Douglas-Home. Wilson was elected largely on the promise of creating a second industrial revolution in Britain, which he called 'the white heat of technological revolution'. The Wilson years saw the fruition of the programme to create new universities and polytechnics, the advent of comprehensive schools, and the building of new housing estates and tower blocks in place of inner-city slums: measures designed to create greater equality of opportunity and an improved standard of living for all. But the technological revolution did not

——PUSHING AT THE BOUNDARIES—— OF MEANING

One of the most striking features of A Clockwork Orange *is the language used by Alex and his fellow 'nadsats' (teenagers). This is a hybrid of Russian and English, described in the novel as 'Odd bits of old rhyming slang…A bit of gypsy talk, too. But most of the roots are Slav. Propaganda. Subliminal penetration.' Burgess fused the two languages with great ingenuity and wit, as the following examples show:*

Gloopy	*Stupid*	*Russian: glupiyi/ foolish, stupid*
Gulliver	*Head*	*Russian: golova/head*
Horrowshow	*Good or Well*	*Russian: khorosho*
Lewdies	*People*	*Russian: lyudi/people*
Nadsat	*Teenage*	*Russian: ending for ages 11-19 (as in —teen)*
Neezhnies	*Underpants*	*Russian: zhniyi/ lower (adj.)*
Oddy-knocky	*Lonesome*	*Russian: odinok/ lonesome*

Similar experiments with language to create a strong sense of conflicts within society can be found in William Golding's The Inheritors *(1955), which describes a moment in pre-history when Cro-Magnon man displaces Neanderthal man, and in Russell Hoban's (1925-)* Riddley Walker *(1980), set in Kent 2000 years after a nuclear holocaust. The narrator speaks in a reconstructed English as he tries to make sense of the remnants of civilisation that he encounters.*

materialise, and the second half of the sixties saw successive economic crises and an increase in industrial unrest. There was a widespread sense of disappointment with Britain's government at home, as well as with its failure to condemn American aggression in Vietnam. Literature, films, journalism and, particularly, drama, began to reflect the view that the old problems of the inter-war years had not been overcome after all.

The permissive society

The Wilson government, which was re-elected in 1966, did however institute a series of permissive measures, broadly reflecting Britain's changing social climate. These included the 1967 Sexual Offences Act which decriminalised homosexual practices between consenting adults (although the age of consent was set at 21, five years older than that governing heterosexual relations); the 1967 Abortion Act, which extended the grounds on which women could legally seek termination; and the 1969 Divorce Reform Act, which relaxed the conditions surrounding the ending of marriage. Racial discrimination in housing and employment was outlawed, although in practice the legislation proved largely ineffective.

Progressive legislation and the new liberalism in society brought with them new freedoms but also new responsibilities, as moral judgements were shifted from the state to the individual. Some writers examined the dilemmas these new freedoms posed, particularly for women. After the predominantly masculine culture of the 1950s novel, the 1960s showed a growing confidence of women writers to voice their own concerns. The early novels of Margaret Drabble (1939-), which include *A Summer Birdcage* (1963), *The Garrick Year* (1964) and *The Millstone* (1965), deal primarily with the dilemma of educated young women caught between the conflicting claims of maternity, sexuality and intellectual and economic aspirations. *A Summer Birdcage* concerns two sisters who are well educated but face the prospect of not being able to get suitable jobs, and of having to work out an attitude towards the 'bird-cage' of marriage. Women readers could recognise their own situation in Drabble's novels. Her heroines are aware of all the traps but uncertain about the new possibilities open to them; on the brink of liberation, but by no means free.

The Golden Notebook (1962) by Doris Lessing (1919-) was hailed as a landmark by the emerging women's movement. It is a lengthy and ambitious book in which sections of conventional narrative, ironically entitled 'Free Women', enclose and intersperse the four experimental notebooks of writer Anna Wulf, who is struggling with crises in her domestic and personal life as well as with writer's block. In each notebook she approaches experience from a different angle, reflecting her sense of fragmentation and need to keep aspects of life in separate compartments. Taken together, the novel presents a critique of the 'sex war', women's liberation, commitment to political action, socialism in England, art and mental breakdown.

Another startling new female voice in the 1960s was that of Muriel Spark (1918-), one of Britain's leading post-war novelists. Her first novel was *The Comforters*, published in 1957, but she is best known for *The Prime of Miss Jean Brodie* (1961), a portrait of an Edinburgh schoolmistress and her group of favoured pupils. The novel starts off in a relatively lighthearted manner, but this changes as parallels between Miss Brodie and the fascist dictators she admires become more apparent, and Miss Brodie's corrupting influence leads to disaster. Spark's novels, which also include *Memento Mori* (1959), *The Ballad of Peckham Rye* (1960) and *The Girls of Slender Means* (1963), often have touches of the bizarre and the perverse. Like those of William Golding (see page 24) and Iris Murdoch (see page 21), they explore the dark side of human nature in a post-war, post-holocaust age, where religion is no longer enough to provide an explanation for human behaviour.

The impact of drama

In theatre and literature, regional, working-class realism and the work of the 'angry young men' (see page 19) continued to dominate in the early 1960s. As well as John Osborne, playwrights such as Arnold Wesker (1932-) dramatised class attitudes in their plays. But in the period around 1963 there was a cultural revolution which affected British drama more than any other literary form. It was in drama, written for film and television as well as for the stage, that the most striking innovations were made. The 1960s is often seen as the richest decade in post-war drama. New regional theatres were built, the Royal Shakespeare Company expanded its operations beyond Stratford and the National Theatre company was founded (although the National Theatre building itself was not opened until 1976). Censorship was abolished, apart from in the cinema. The turbulence of the times seemed to breed exciting theatre. Drama, like society, was in a state of transition, and theatre played a vital part in the debates about what shape the new society would take.

Some dramatists in the 1960s used the theme of disintegrating families as a metaphor for the way society was falling apart and re-ordering itself. In *A Day in the Death of Joe Egg* (1967), Peter Nichols (1927-) uses marriage and the struggle of bringing up a handicapped child to explore society's moral confusion over the right to take life. In *Celebration* (1969), David Storey (1933-) explores guilt, secrecy and the generation gap between three educated sons and their miner father in a Yorkshire mining community.

Two of the most original and challenging of the new dramatists who came to prominence in 1960s were Harold Pinter and Joe Orton (1933-67). Pinter, who came from the East End of London, trained as an actor before becoming a playwright. He began writing plays in the late 1950s – *The Room*, *The Dumb Waiter* and *The Birthday Party* were all written in 1957 – and he was also a critic and director. Of his prolific output, two of the plays considered to be among his most significant are *The Caretaker* (1960) and *The Homecoming* (1965). Neither of these 'comedies of menace' are overtly political, but they open up a world of dislocated relationships and tangential communication where events seem inconsequential and there is a constant feeling of undefined threat. Like those of Beckett (see page 16), Pinter's plays are famous for the use they make of silences between characters.

The Homecoming, which was first performed by the newly formed Royal Shakespeare Company in 1965, takes its title from the return to London of Teddy, an academic working in America, and his wife Ruth, who grew up in the same area as Teddy's family. Teddy's father, Max, is a foul-mouthed bigot who bullies and manipulates his other sons Joey and Lenny in turns. Pinter creates a whole world of vague menace behind the simple conversations that take place between the characters, but the action on stage is equally disturbing: by the end of the play Ruth has taken the role of prostitute and surrogate mother and Teddy returns to America. The play paints a bleak and shocking picture of family relationships without any possibility of improvement.

Joe Orton

Joe Orton was a writer of strikingly original black comedies, whose life and work represent the struggle of permissiveness and anarchy against authority in the 1960s. His five major plays, which were produced at the Royal Court Theatre, are *Entertaining Mr Sloane* (1964), *Loot* (1966), *The Ruffian on the Stair*, *The Erpingham Camp* (both 1967) and the posthumously produced *What the Butler Saw* (1968). Orton was a promiscuous homosexual in a period when sexual acts between consenting males were still regarded as a criminal offence. At the age of 31 he was murdered by his partner and occasional collaborator, Kenneth Halliwell. In 1962 Orton and Halliwell had been prosecuted for stealing and defacing library books, and sent to prison by a particularly authoritarian magistrate. Orton fought back against authority in his writing with the use of anarchic comedy and sexual innuendo. What his plays communicate is an indiscriminate scorn for human institutions and values, and a scathing pleasure in exposing them as corrupt or hypocritical. Orton celebrates a world which he saw as 'profoundly bad but irresistibly funny'.

Orton exploited existing theatrical forms, including techniques learnt from traditional British farce, but he also transformed them to suit the dangerous spirit of his writing. Whereas in traditional farce order is restored at the end of the play, the endings of Orton's plays reinforce and sustain moral chaos. Throwaway lines such as 'We must keep up appearances' (*Loot*), or 'I'm glad you don't despise tradition. Let us put our clothes on and face the world' (*What the Butler Saw*) use linguistic conventions and social nicety simply to subvert the idea of social order. But Orton's plays are also profoundly serious. In *Loot*, for example, the figure of police-inspector Truscott directly refers to a real police officer, detective-sergeant Harold Challenor, who was tried for corruption. The following exchange between Truscott and a man he is arresting shows how Orton challenges assumptions of law and order, destroying the notion of the police as an agency of social cohesion and justice (as it was represented, for example, in the popular television drama series *Dixon of Dock Green*):

MCLEAVY: What am I charged with?
TRUSCOTT: That needn't concern you for the moment. We'll fill in the details later.
MCLEAVY: You can't do this. I've always been a law-abiding citizen. The police are for the protection of ordinary people.
TRUSCOTT: I don't know where you pick up these slogans, sir. You must read them on hoardings.

Orton's last play, *What the Butler Saw*, is set in a private psychiatric clinic where insanity is exploited rather than cured. The title draws the audience's attention to the cultural clichés from music hall and traditional British entertainment such as farce and Victorian peepshow machines that Orton employs. The farce includes plenty of sexual titillation, cross-dressing and disguise, and mistaken identity as the tempo of the action winds ever quicker. But the play, like Orton's others, is also an uncompromising attack on authority figures such as Winston Churchill, the police sergeant and the government inspector.

Television drama

More than in any other decade, television drama in the 1960s offered a genuine opportunity for writers with serious social and aesthetic purposes to reach a mass audience. BBC 2 began broadcasting in 1964, widening the scope of television to present arts programmes and documentaries as well as drama. The BBC's *Wednesday Play* series, which ran from 1964 to 1970, was particularly influential in bringing radical and innovative drama to a mass audience. Nell Dunn (1936-) was a member of the 'swinging London' scene, but her novels *Up the Junction* (1963) and *Poor Cow* (1967), were concerned with working-class women and helped contribute to a new openness about female sexuality. The title of *Up the Junction* is a pun, connoting both pregnancy and the working-class south London area of Clapham Junction. When it was shown as part of the *Wednesday Play* series in 1965, directed by Ken Loach, it caused an outcry for its abortion scene. Dunn and Loach co-wrote a screenplay of *Poor Cow* in 1968; the film was a hit but lost much of its radicalism in its translation to the big screen.

Cathy Come Home (1966) was another ground-breaking *Wednesday Play*. The story of *Cathy Come Home*, written by Jeremy Sandford and again directed by Ken Loach, concerns a young mother forced to move from one squalid lodging to another, then taken into a hostel for the homeless before finally being evicted and having her children taken away from her. It broke with film convention in the way in which it combined naturalistic acting, true-to-life characterisation and situation with an observational camera style and voice-over narration, giving a documentary quality to the drama. This documentary style, together with the subject matter, caused a sensation when *Cathy Come Home* was first screened, and it became probably the only television drama directly to affect social policy: as a result of the play and its critical reception, the pressure group Shelter was set up.

Pop culture – swinging London

During the 1960s the post-war 'baby boom' generation was growing up, creating a powerful new army of consumers. Society as a whole was offered greater opportunities and freedoms than ever before, and within that society individuals and groups, including youth, the working class and – to a lesser extent – women and ethnic minorities, all became more visible and assertive. The power of advertising, particularly on television, led to the birth of mass-consumerism. For the first time, fashion, furniture, cars, music and cinema were all aimed at the newly affluent youth market. 'Swinging London' was the centre of an emerging pop culture and Britain, which during the 1950s had been seen as a backwater in the face of the ever-faster spread of American culture, seemed for a while to be setting the pace.

Pop music was the essence of the cultural revolution in the 1960s. The music of bands such as the Beatles and the Rolling Stones came to symbolise young audiences' rejection of parental values. Working-class rebellion was symbolised by the Mods, with their sharp suits, parkas, Lambretta scooters and violent clashes with Rockers on bank holiday beaches. The Mod band The Who expressed their triumph in the song 'My Generation', claiming,

'Hope I die before I get old!' Meanwhile, their middle-class contemporaries were influenced by San Francisco and the 'mystical' east. The hippies of 1966 and 1967 grew their hair long, proclaimed peace and love and discovered themselves through psychedelic drugs, rock festivals and free love (meaning free sex). Eastern-oriented music and 'flower-power' as well as underground magazines such as *Oz* and *International Times* were all part of the hippy counter-culture prevalent among students.

Cinema

Nowhere were the cultural tensions of the decade represented more vividly than in the cinema. The decline in attendances caused by the desertion of the regular family audience to television had a liberating effect, causing the industry to take risks with a wider range of themes, styles, and personnel. The breakthrough of *Room at the Top* (see page 20) was followed by a series of films set in the industrial Midlands or north of England, which refused to compromise the radical vision of the contemporary plays and novels on which they were based; an important part of their strategy was to introduce new stars like Albert Finney (*Saturday Night and Sunday Morning*, 1960), Rita Tushingham (*A Taste of Honey*, 1961), and Tom Courtenay (*Billy Liar*, 1963), whose appeal was precisely that they retained the rough edges and regional accents that the industry would previously have insisted on smoothing away. But the cinema's centre of gravity inevitably soon shifted back southward, along with its new directors and actors, drawn into the vortex of pop culture and 'swinging London'. The exuberant energy of this period is captured in films as varied as the period romp *Tom Jones* (1963, with Albert Finney), the first Beatles film *A Hard Day's Night* (1964), and *Darling* (1965), which earned Julie Christie an Oscar for her portayal of a sexually liberated child of her times.

Poetry: old and new

The mood of the 1960s was one of rebellion – in the quest for self-expression, for liberation, for 'doing your own thing'. Like artists and musicians, poets experimented with new forms and new kinds of subject matter, seeking what was for them most truthful and most alive to contemporary experience. In the introduction to his anthology *The New Poetry* (1962), poet and critic Al Alvarez attacked established forms and values, arguing that English poets, bound by the decency and politeness of the English tradition, had failed to come to terms with the 'forces of disintegration' at work in man, forces whose 'public faces are those of two world wars, of the concentration camps, of genocide, and the threat of nuclear war'. Alvarez claimed that some of the English and American poets included in his anthology, such as Ted Hughes and Sylvia Plath,

If **(1968)**
Directed by Lindsay Anderson

One of the finest films of the decade, before the industry
was overtaken by financial crisis, was Lindsay Anderson's
If, which used a public school setting for a savage fable of
youthful rebellion against the Establishment. The film ends
with a group of boys launching an attack (shown in this
still) on parents and pupils at Speech Day, using grenades
and machine guns found under the school stage.

were aware of those forces in a way that the 'genteel' poetry of Philip Larkin was not:

> I am not suggesting that modern English poetry, to be really modern, must be concerned with psychoanalysis or with the concentration camps or with the hydrogen bomb or with any other of the modern horrors. I am not suggesting, in fact, that it *must* be anything. For poetry that feels it has to cope with pre-determined subjects ceases to be poetry and becomes propaganda. I am, however, suggesting that it drop the pretence that life, give or take a few social distinctions, is the same as ever, that gentility, decency and all the other social totems will eventually muddle through.

The poetry of Philip Larkin and his fellow Movement poets (see page 19) typified for Alvarez all that was wrong with English poetry but nevertheless, Larkin's work was and remains very popular with both critics and the general public. Larkin, who was born in Coventry, became a librarian after leaving Oxford University, and remained a working librarian until retirement despite becoming one of Britain's foremost literary figures. Early in his career he wrote two novels, *Jill* (1946) and *A Girl in Winter* (1947), as well as a later collection of essays, *All What Jazz* (1970), but his reputation rests on three volumes of poetry: *The Less Deceived* (1955), *The Whitsun Weddings* (1964) and *High Windows* (1974). In keeping with the Movement's anti-heroic, anti-romantic attitude, his writing emphasises simple truths about life, and deliberately plays down the glamour of situations and people, replacing sentimentality with a dry, matter-of-fact approach and

— POP ART —

The term 'Pop Art' was first used by the English critic Lawrence Alloway in a 1958 issue of the Architectural Digest *to describe paintings that celebrated post-war consumerism, defied the psychology of Abstract Expressionism in art, and worshipped the gods of materialism. Pop Art brought art back to the material realities of everyday life, in which ordinary people derived most of their visual pleasure from television, magazines or comics. The media and advertising were the favourite subjects for Pop Art's often witty celebrations of consumer society. Pop artists sought to give the same amount of significance to everyday, mass-produced objects as to the epic subjects of classical art: their aim was to close the gap between 'high' and 'low' culture.*

Pop Art first emerged in Britain in the mid-1950s, where one of its leading exponents was Richard Hamilton (1922-). His 1956 montage of magazine imagery entitled Just what is it that makes today's homes so different, so appealing?, *in which cut-outs of a muscle-man and a nude girl occupy a room equipped with all modern conveniences is now an iconic Pop Art image. David Hockney's (1937-) early paintings, with their use of popular magazine-style images, also gained him a reputation as a leading pop artist, although he himself rejected the label. Hockney travelled to America in the 1960s, and created a series of swimming pool paintings which celebrate the male nude, including* A Bigger Splash *(1967). One of Hockney's most popular works is* Mr and Mrs Clark and Percy *(1970), a portrait of the 'swinging London' fashion designer Ossie Clark and his wife Celia Birtwell with their cat. Another British pop artist, Peter Blake (1932-), whose work in the 1960s evoked a nostalgia for childhood memories and favourite television and film stars, is probably best known for his 1967 album cover design for the Beatles' 'Sergeant Pepper's Lonely Hearts Club Band'. The Pop Art movement quickly made its way to the United States and reached its peak in New York during the 1960s with the work of Claes Oldenburg and Roy Lichtenstein as well as that of its most famous exponent, Andy Warhol (1928-87).*

_____

***Mr and Mrs Clark and Percy* (1970), David Hockney (above);
Album cover for 'Sergeant Pepper's Lonely Hearts Club Band' (1967)**

Two examples of images from the Pop Art movement. The artist Richard Hamilton summarised the main features of Pop Art in the following words: 'Popular...; Transient...; Low Cost; Mass Produced; Young...; Witty; Sexy; Gimmicky; Glamorous; Big Business'.

stoic wit. The poems collected in *The Whitsun Weddings* present a range of melancholy urban and suburban landscapes and a lightly satirical commentary on contemporary life from the 1950s as much as the 1960s. In 'Afternoons' he observes a group of young mothers with their children in a public park set among 'estatefuls of washing':

> Their beauty has thickened;
> Something is pushing them
> To the side of their own lives.

The title poem of the collection is typical of Larkin's poetry in that he stands apart from the scenes he describes, alienated from the 'parodies of fashion', the 'uncle shouting smut' and the 'bunting-dressed coach-party annexes', but at the very end of the poem there is a sense of something more hopeful in the image of 'an arrow-shower/ sent out of sight, somewhere becoming rain.'

In one of his best-known poems, 'Annus Mirabilis' (published in his 1974 collection, *High Windows*), Larkin refers to the paperback publication of *Lady Chatterley's Lover* as part of a wider shift in popular culture and manners:

> Sexual intercourse began
> In nineteen sixty-three
> (Which was rather late for me)-
> Between the end of the Chatterley ban
> And the Beatles' first LP.

The most powerful voice in British poetry during the 1960s was that of Ted Hughes (1930-98), who had enjoyed immediate critical success in 1957 with *Hawk in the Rain*, followed by *Lupercal* in 1960. Hughes was to be the dominant poetic voice in the following two decades, becoming Poet Laureate in 1984 on the death of John Betjeman. He was married to the American writer Sylvia Plath, who had a significant, if largely unrecognised, influence on *Hawk in the Rain*. Until their marriage broke up both poets fed off each others' thoughts and ideas, and Plath's posthumous collection *Ariel*

—THE END OF CENSORSHIP—

Lady Chatterley's Lover *(1928), the long-banned novel by D.H. Lawrence (1885-1930), emerged from the shadows and into the bookshops in 1960, thanks to a landmark decision by a jury at the Old Bailey. The book, which contained explicit description of sexual acts and equally explicit language, was prosecuted under the 1959 Obscene Publications Act, but was judged not to be obscene. The trial generated so much interest that 200,000 copies of* Lady Chatterley's Lover, *which was published in paperback by Penguin, were sold in one day. The Lady Chatterley trial was a test case for the new Act, the first of its kind since 1857, which was designed to draw a line between 'filth' and work that, though controversial, was considered to be of genuine literary merit. In many ways the trial pitted the old Britain against the new, with experts from both sides putting forward their own sincerely held beliefs. It was not only a case of what makes 'literature', but of the direction of national morality. The question asked of the jury by the prosecuting counsel in the case, to the effect of whether or not the jury would allow one of their wives or servants to read such a novel, has become famous as a symbol of an age that was already past in 1960. In the event, the jury's decision was significant because it marked an effective end to book censorship in Britain, and paved the way for the ending of other forms of censorship. In 1968, on the day after the censorship of the Lord Chamberlain over the theatre was finally abolished, the hippy musical* Hair, *in which the cast appeared naked at the end of the first act, opened on the London stage.*

(1965) revealed a highly original voice, powerful and dramatic in its depiction of mortality and the edges of sanity. Hughes's main preoccupations were with the untamed forces of nature and their interaction with man, rather than the suburban world of shops, trains and hospitals discussed in Larkin's poetry. Hughes's early poems reveal a fascination with animal energy and independence, and an awareness of the affinities between animal and human life, between human aspirations to freedom and power and the instinctive animal achievement of both. The brutality of nature in poems such as 'Pike' or 'Thrushes' can be read allegorically as the writer's growing concern with violence in the 20th century. Although the anger and violence of Hughes's poetry seems directly at odds with the sardonic, gently despairing bitterness of Larkin, the poetry of both men shares a common sense of alienation.

The enduringly popular Liverpool poets Roger McGough (1937-, Adrian Henri (1932-2000) and Brian Patten (1946-), sought to close the gap between popular music and poetry. They wanted to bring poetry back to its folk roots by emphasising that poetry, like pop music, should be performed in public before a live audience. Other British poets such as Adrian Mitchell (1932-) and Michael Horovitz (1935-) modelled themselves on the American beat poets who were exploring the links between poetry and jazz.

End of the 'swinging sixties'

By 1968 – the year when students and workers rioted in Paris and nearly overthrew the French government, and when the anti-Vietnam war movement came to a head in America – the youthful optimism of the early to mid-1960s had all but vanished. There were protests against the British government's decision to send troops to Northern Ireland, where the civil rights campaign among Catholics in Derry and Belfast had escalated into riots and civil unrest unparalleled for 50 years.

Ironically, the 'swinging sixties' ended as they had begun, with the trial of a publication – but this time the publishers were found guilty of obscenity. The underground magazine, *Oz*, had offered schoolchildren the chance to put together a whole issue, and the offer was taken up with great vigour: the resulting 'Schoolkids Oz' included among its controversial contents a cartoon of Rupert Bear involved in a sexual act. The prosecution's case rested largely on the involvement and possible corruption of young people; the publishers were given lengthy prison sentences, but were released on appeal. The *Oz* trial represented the paradox at the heart of British culture and society in the 1960s: an apparently liberated decade, in which the values of the old Establishment appeared to have been overturned, but where the libertarian spirit did not ultimately run very deep.

4. THE END OF IDEALISM (1970-79)

The drive for 'liberation' that had begun in the 1960s continued in the following decade, and in many ways the new lifestyles and cultural changes which came into being in the 1960s became absorbed into the fabric of society. But it was also a time of worldwide terrorist outrages, and of economic difficulties throughout the Western world. Political events, including the American war in Vietnam, the Soviet invasion of Czechoslovakia in 1968, and the French student/workers protest in the same year had resulted in increasing militancy in Britain from working-class organisations and trade unions, students and the 'New Left'. From these tumultuous events, which carried on until the early 1970s, emerged opposing notions of culture, history and society. In the course of the 1970s many people turned away from trying to change the world to concentrate instead on changing themselves. In what was later dubbed the 'me decade', self-expression and self-liberation, aided by a boom in self-help books and alternative therapies, became widely pursued goals.

Industrial unrest

Although living standards were higher than ever before, the British economy continued to decline throughout the 1970s, unaffected by an alternation of power between Labour and Conservative governments. The Conservatives swept into office in the 1970 general election under the leadership of Edward Heath, whose regime was markedly to the right of previous Tory administrations. Newcomers to cabinet office included Margaret Thatcher as Secretary of State for Education.

By the early 1970s Britain was embroiled in industrial unrest, and in a divisive debate on membership of the European Community. Heath had been negotiating to join the EEC for over a decade (a previous attempt by Harold Macmillan was thwarted by General de Gaulle of France) and finally got his way in 1973, when Britain joined the Community along with Ireland, Denmark and Norway. At the same time, Heath was confronted by a damaging miners' strike, widespread trade union militancy, and a drastic surge in the price of oil in the aftermath of the Arab-Israeli Yom Kippur war in the Middle East. Matters came to a head late in 1973, and Heath announced a set of emergency measures reminiscent of 1940s austerity. Most workers would go on a three-day week, there would be a general speed limit of 50mph (80km/h), and television broadcasts would end at 10.30 pm. These measures were supposed to save fuel, but the result was to make people depressed and angry. Heath's attempts to deal with the trade unions failed, and in 1974 Labour returned to power, still under the leadership of Harold Wilson.

Instead of relying on legislation to curb strikes, as the Conservatives had done, the Wilson government introduced a voluntary 'social contract' with the unions. This was not a success, and by the mid-'70s unemployment figures had passed the two million mark, a level unknown since the 1930s. In April 1976 Wilson shocked the country, and his own party, by abruptly resigning as prime minister. He was succeeded by James Callaghan, whose new cabinet was immediately confronted with a grave economic crisis. The value of the pound sank, the trade deficit soared and the government had to borrow heavily from the International Monetary Fund. In late 1978, public services were hit by a series of strikes, causing a 'winter of discontent' as miserable as Heath's three-day week of 1973-74. Rubbish piled up in the streets and even gravediggers went on strike. Callaghan was attacked by the new Conservative leader Margaret Thatcher, who described his deals with the unions as a 'boneless wonder'.

Silver Jubilee

The Queen's Silver Jubilee in 1977 saw a very different Britain, and a very different national mood, from that of the period of her accession in 1952 and her coronation a year later. Although there were lively public celebrations to mark the Jubilee, there was also widespread recognition that in the previous 25 years Britain's role in the world had changed radically, and that the process of adjustment to these changes was not proving easy. Almost all the colonies that made up the former British Empire had now achieved full independence; the 'special relationship' with the USA, strengthened by the wartime alliance, was becoming harder to sustain; and involvement in the European Community remained at best half-hearted. Although the country had shared in the general growth of prosperity during the 1950s and 1960s, by the time of the Jubilee it had slipped steadily down the world's economic league tables. Britain could take credit for the smooth transfer of power which transformed an Empire into an equal 'Commonwealth' of nations, and it remained one of the world's few nuclear powers, but the words of the American statesman Dean Acheson were hard to dispute: Britain 'had lost an Empire, and not yet found a role'.

Women's liberation

The most important protest movement of the 1970s was women's liberation, as the women's movement was then known. Women fought for an equal right to jobs and to promotion, and for equal pay when they did the same work as men. Feminists protested against beauty contests and pin-up photos that showed women as sex objects, as well as demanding that men should do an equal share of housework and other chores. In Britain women's rights made two tangible advances in 1970 in terms of law reform. The Matrimonial Property Act required a wife's work – whether in jobs outside the home or as a housewife within it – to be regarded as an equal contribution with that of her husband, if, in the event of divorce, the family home had to be divided. The Equal Pay Act, which only came fully into practice in 1975, finally established the principle of equal pay for equal work. Feminists welcomed both these acts, which continued the process of reform which gathered momentum during the 1960s in areas such as divorce, abortion and contraception. The availability of the contraceptive pill came to symbolise a new liberation for women, which Germaine Greer (1939-) advanced in her bestselling book *The Female Eunuch*, published in 1970. Greer challenged the masculine world with an erudite critique of the way it stereotyped women's roles.

A distinctive feature of the women's movement was the close relationship between theory and practice. Women's writing, even avowedly non-feminist writing, in the 1970s tended to focus on themes of motherhood, the contradictions of women's roles, and an often confessional search for 'authentic' experiences which reflected the politics of the women's movement and the theorising of academic feminists like Germaine Greer. The women's magazine *Spare Rib*, launched in 1972, was both a product of and a feminist reaction to the 'alternative' magazines of the sixties – which hardly addressed women and were often blatantly sexist – as well as an alternative to commercial women's magazines. The politics underlying *Spare Rib* were those of moving away from the 'personal liberation' of sixties counterculture to engage in the politics of femininity. Its mission was to explain the politics of the women's

— GOD SAVE THE QUEEN —

By the early '70s British pop music had fragmented into many different genres. At one end of the spectrum there was pure pop played by glam rock bands like the Sweet and teenybop bands like the Bay City Rollers; at the other end were bands such as Yes who used forms from classical music and sought musical respectability. Roxy Music and David Bowie used dress and make-up as well as choreographed stage performances to create a new kind of musical performance art. The major new movement which began in the USA in 1975 and soon spread its influence worldwide was disco music. The disco boom peaked three years later with the enormously successful Hollywood film Saturday Night Fever.

In 1976 the world of pop was turned upside down by punk; the first musical genre since rock and roll in the 1950s successfully to alienate parents and give expression to young people disillusioned by a society that had failed to live up to their expectations. The first, and archetypal, British punk band was the Sex Pistols, guided by fashion entrepreneur Malcolm McLaren in partnership with designer Vivienne Westwood. Punk music was simple, loud, fast, aggressive and raw. But punk was more than music: it was also a new subculture – this time one which involved girls as full participants rather than as accessories. Committed to 'anarchy', punks set out to shock with their frightening appearance and image: dyed Mohican hairstyles, bondage gear, ripped t-shirts and pierced bodies. Swearing on television was strictly taboo in the 1970s, and the Sex Pistols caused an outrage on the Thames Today *programme for using the 'f word' several times in the course of a live interview with Bill Grundy, which was abruptly terminated. In 1976 their anti-jubilee single (re-released in 2002 to mark the Queen's Golden Jubilee), containing the lyrics 'God save the Queen/the fascist regime' was banned by the BBC. Although punk lived on as a subculture, many of the brash young bands of the punk movement, like The Police and U2, became part of the new musical establishment. When the Sex Pistols' Sid Vicious died in 1979, it signalled the end of the punk era.*

Sid Vicious of the punk band the Sex Pistols
The band was fronted by John Lydon, known as Johnny Rotten.

movement in an accessible way, and to some extent it succeeded, although it never achieved anything approaching the popularity of mainstream 'glossies' like *Cosmopolitan*, launched the same year.

The early 1970s also saw the emergence of feminist, or women-centred, publishing companies. Virago Press was founded in 1973, and followed by a stream of other women's presses such as Pandora, the Women's Press and Sheba. The aim of Virago's Modern Classics series was 'to demonstrate the existence of a female literary tradition and to broaden the sometimes narrow definition of a classic.' The series was launched in 1977 with *Frost in May* by Antonia White (1899-1979), which had faded into obscurity after its first publication in 1933. Virago was also responsible for introducing contemporary women writers such as Angela Carter (1940-92) and Margaret Atwood (1939-). The women's presses changed the face of publishing and, to some extent, of literature in the 1970s, encouraging and responding to women's growing political consciousness. By the '80s, however, the independent woman had become a buoyant consumer market and, after a series of take-overs, feminist publishing went mainstream.

Angela Carter is the most celebrated feminist writer of the period, although she is equally well known for her association with a style of writing known as magic realism, (see Glossary of Terms) which she first used in *The Magic Toyshop* (1967). As well as writing fiction, she was a journalist and critic. Much of her writing draws on the symbolism and themes of children's fairy tales and folk myths, but her stories, which are imbued with macabre fantasy and erotic comedy, are for adult readers. In her many-layered, shifting narratives there is no distinction between probable people and improbable ones, or between humans and animals. Carter's feminist concerns, which underpin all her writing, are perhaps most explicit in *The Passion of New Eve* (1977). The novel, which explores the constructed nature of gender, is set in a horrifically violent America of the near future. A good-looking, predatory man is captured by a women's group and subjected to an operation which turns him into a highly desirable but vulnerable young woman. But although Carter is strongly identified as a feminist writer, much of her writing takes issue with some expressions of feminist thought in the 1970s, particularly those that rely on depictions of women as victims of a patriarchal society. Instead, she explores domination and submission in sexual relationships. Her 1979 essay *The Sadeian Woman and the Ideology of Pornography* explores her sometimes troubled relationship with feminism, and her interest in the politics of sex. *The Bloody Chamber and Other Stories* (1979) contains reworkings of the stories of Bluebeard, Beauty and the Beast, Puss in Boots and Little Red Riding Hood, while *Nights At The Circus* (1984) is the bawdy, but at the same time serious, story of Fevvers, a Victorian music-hall artist who has wings. All of Carter's writing is at odds with conventional realism, yet at the same time feminist critics perceived that it created a 'realistic' map of female fantasy.

Another name linked with the Virago press is that of the Canadian writer Margaret Atwood. Her novels of the period, which include *The Edible Woman* (1969), *Surfacing* (1972). *Lady Oracle* (1976) and *Life Before Man* (1979), established Atwood as one of the most critically acclaimed and popular writers of her generation. Like Angela Carter, Atwood is a writer who often plays with fairy tale images in her work. 'The Robber Bridegroom' (which she much later turned on its head with *The Robber Bride,* 1993), was one of the inspirations for *The Edible Woman*. The old crone in the story warns bride-to-be Marian 'The only marriage you'll celebrate will be with death… When they have you in their power they'll chop you up in pieces… then they'll cook you and eat you, because they are cannibals.' *Lady Oracle*, Atwood's third novel, is also a comedy which parodies literary forms and subverts literary expectations. Like *The Edible Woman*, one of *Lady Oracle*'s themes is women's relationship with food and obesity. After the 1970s Atwood's novels become more serious in tone. The *Handmaid's Tale* (1985) is a futuristic fable, set in the imaginary Republic of Gilead, about a woman whose only function is to breed. It was followed by *Cat's Eye* (1989), *Alias Grace* (1996), and *The Blind Assassin* (2000).

The novels of Fay Weldon (1931-) also express the rising feminist consciousness of the 1970s. She explores women's troubled relationships with parents, men and children and with one another, often using a tragi-comic tone. Weldon is particularly noted for her realistic dialogue, and her use of running commentary. One of the characters in *Down Among the Women* (1971) states: 'Down among the women. What a place to be! Yet here we are by accident of birth, sprouted breast and bellies, as cyclical of nature as our timekeeper the moon – and down here among the women we have no option but to stay.' The heroine of *Female Friends* (1975) is affectionate, loyal and bewildered: she is the imposed-upon victim of female friends and a bullying husband. She wins the reader's sympathy for not being liberated, and yet seems to learn at the end that it is time to break out. A central thread of Weldon's writing is an emphasis on biology as a major determinant for gender, as in *Puffball* (1980) which contrasts medical descriptions of the female body during menstruation, taking the contraceptive pill and pregnancy, with a storyline about marital infidelity.

Many of the other most memorable novels of the decade came from women who did not, however, identify themselves explicitly as feminists. *The Sea, The Sea*, which won the Booker Prize for Iris Murdoch (see page 21) in 1978, is arguably the purest distillation of her powers as a romantic visionary and as a story teller. In it, a male theatre director retires to a life of orderly solitude by the sea, only to find himself assailed by figures from the past, including his long-lost first love, whom he feels compelled to reclaim. The previous year had seen the rediscovery of Barbara Pym (1913-80), whose *Quartet in Autumn*, short-listed for the 1977 Booker Prize, inspired the reprinting of her backlist of sharp comedies of English middle-class life; *Quartet* itself is more melancholy, a delicate and touching account of a quartet of linked individuals declining gently into old age. A younger, equally idiosyncratic female voice was that of Beryl Bainbridge (1934-). Her novels of the period include *The Dressmaker* (1973), *The Bottle Factory Outing* (1974), *Sweet William* (1975) and *Injury Time* (1977). Bainbridge uses black comedy to deal with the lives of characters who are both ordinary and eccentric, in a world where violence and the absurd lurk beneath the routine of urban domesticity. In *Injury Time*, for example, a quietly illicit dinner party becomes headline news when invaded by a gang of criminals on the run who take its guests hostage.

The campus novel

Among male novelists, Kingsley Amis (see page 21) continued, like Murdoch, to produce novels at a consistent rate and to a familiar pattern. But the novel that came more than any other to epitomise the decade was *The History Man* (1975) by Malcolm Bradbury (1932-2000). Bradbury was a professor at one of the new universities of the 1960s, the University of East Anglia in Norwich, and the founder of a pioneer postgraduate programme in creative writing that would have a significant influence on the subsequent development of the English novel; set at a fictional university of the same vintage, *The History Man* follows the adventures of a ruthless and trendy sociologist, Howard Kirk, who is equally skilled at manipulating students, colleagues, lovers and the media. The book's success in bringing a new kind of modern institution into public consciousness was reinforced by its adaptation as a TV serial soon afterwards.

Malcolm Bradbury's name is usually coupled with that of David Lodge (1935-) as the leading writers of the so-called 'campus novels', following in the traditions of Amis's *Lucky Jim* (see page 21) in depicting the lives and follies of academics in a university setting. Lodge's comedies *Changing Places* (1975) and *Small World* (1984) focus on Philip Swallow, from the University of Birmingham (which Lodge renames Rummidge) who takes part in an exchange with Maurice Zapp from Euphoria State University, while *Nice Work* (1989) has as its main character Robyn Penrose, who shadows the boss of a local engineering firm in Rummidge to compare working practices.

Angela Carter
Much of Carter's writing shows the influence of fantasy, fairy tale
and feminism. Her later work (she died at the relatively young
age of 52) was more conventional in its setting and plot than
her earlier fiction, though it is still clearly artificial: Carter was a
leading exponent of magic realism (see Glossary of Terms), and
in her work, the reader can take little for granted.

Northern Ireland: the 'Troubles'

In Northern Ireland, deep-seated racial and religious animosities between Protestants and Catholics were aggravated by the highest rate of unemployment·in Britain. As the violence escalated in 1971, the Heath government introduced internment without trial, thus provoking further violence in protest. On 30 January 1972, British troops opened fire on civil rights marchers in Derry, killing 13 people. The impact of this violence was so profound that the date became known as 'Bloody Sunday', and 30 years later the event was still the subject of a judicial investigation. Later in 1972 self-government in Northern Ireland was suspended and replaced by direct rule from Westminster. Renewed violence by the IRA was paralleled by the aggressive, anti-Catholic politics of the Reverend Ian Paisley, whose new 'Democratic Unionist Party' was well to the right of the established Unionists. The end of self-government brought peace no nearer, and British troops continued to patrol the streets of West Belfast. Throughout the decade there were violent incidents on the border between Ulster and the Irish Republic to the south, from where the IRA were supplied with funds and weapons. The violence occasionally spread to England, where there were bomb attacks on cities including London and Birmingham, and assassinations of high-profile figures such as the Conservative spokesman on Northern Ireland, Airey Neave, and Lord Mountbatten, a cousin of the Queen. By the end of the decade there was no sign of political progress in Northern Ireland, just endless violence. It was not until 1985 that the Anglo-Irish agreement was signed, providing for increased cross-border co-operation and greater consultation between the British and Irish governments.

The 'Troubles' have been treated in many imaginative ways by Northern Irish writers. Brian Friel (1929-) has written almost exclusively about and for Ireland since the 1960s. In the late '70s he co-founded a touring theatre company called Field Day, together with actor Stephen Rea and the poets Seamus Heaney and Tom Paulin, 'to put on plays outside the confines of established theatre, and through that to begin to effect changes in the apathetic atmosphere of the North.' Friel's plays explore the idea of an independent Ireland, and how Irish culture can survive in a colonised country. *The Freedom of the City* (1973) is set in the dangerous Derry of 1970, as British troops attempt to disperse Catholic civil rights marchers, three of whom take refuge in the Unionist mayor's parlour in the Guildhall. *Aristocrats* (1979) is set in a large and decaying house, where an outsider (Tom, an American academic) is researching the attitudes and politics of the Roman Catholic aristocracy in Ireland. The family he is staying with include a spinster daughter who looks after her senile, incontinent father, a younger daughter who is a brilliant pianist but nervous and on tranquillisers, and a son who has gone to live in Germany but holds on to myths and stories about the family, boasting of its association with almost every famous Irish cultural figure, including Gerard Manley Hopkins and James Joyce. By the end of the play, the family is disintegrating but still held together by rituals and memories.

Translations (1980) is set in a Gaelic-speaking community in County Donegal in the 1830s, where a classics scholar, Hugh, gives lessons at a 'hedge school' (a basic, low-class school for the local community). The play explores the interaction of Irish and English cultures, through the medium of language. *Translations* is written in English, but none of the Irish characters speaks English, although some of them are fluent in Greek and Latin. British soldiers, the agents of colonialism, are making a new map of the area: they set about anglicising 'every hill, stream, rock, even every patch of ground which possesses its own distinctive Irish name'. The play, as its title suggests, is concerned with the importance of language to culture, and about the possibilities of transcending the barrier of language to find a common means of communication. The most moving moment in the play takes place when the English Lieutenant Yolland and one of the locals, Maire, try to express their feelings of love for one another; neither understands the other, but the audience knows what both are saying:

YOLLAND   I wish to God you could understand me.
MAIRE   Soft hands; a gentleman's hands.
YOLLAND   Because if you could understand me I could tell you how I spend my days either thinking of you or gazing up at your house in the hope that you'll appear even for a second.
MAIRE   Every morning you walk by yourself along the Tra Bhan and every morning you wash yourself in front of your tent.
YOLLAND   I would tell you how beautiful you are, curly-headed Maire. I would so like to tell you how beautiful you are.
MAIRE   Your arms are long and thin and the skin on your shoulders is very white.

Making History (1988) explores how the writing of history imposes orderly narrative patterns and a convenient interpretation on material that is essentially disordered and inconclusive. Friel's most celebrated play, *Dancing at Lughnasa* (1990), which was adapted for the cinema, has an adult narrator looking back at his boyhood in Donegal. The play questions the inward-looking values of a tightly knit Catholic family, and also draws out parallels between Catholic culture in rural Ireland and a despised, 'pagan' Africa where the Irish are involved in missionary work.

Seamus Heaney (1939-) grew up in a Catholic farming community in County Derry, Northern Ireland, and the rural Ulster of his childhood figures in much of his verse. His early poetry – *Death of a Naturalist* (1966), *Door into the Dark* (1969), and *Wintering Out* (1972) – was largely autobiographical or concerned with nature, but in the early 1970s he became increasingly involved in the political situation, and his next volume of poems reflects that involvement. *North* (1975) established Heaney as a popular and critical success, selling more copies even than Philip Larkin's *The Whitsun Weddings* or Ted Hughes's *Crow* (1970). The title refers both to the north of Ireland and to other northern civilisations that have shaped and influenced Ireland, particularly those of the Vikings and the English. The title poem, 'North', looks back to Viking Ireland, to the ruthlessness of Norse enterprise, and reflects on how a poet can use a language buried, like alien treasure, in his native soil. Heaney's aim in *North* is to create connections through language, ritual and archaeology between the past and the present, in order to give a cultural and historical context to the sectarian violence of the '60s and '70s.

Heaney sees the rifts in Irish life as rooted in a long history of occupation and imperial influence: 'Freedman', for example, draws parallels between the culture of the Roman (Catholic) church and slavery in ancient Rome, while 'Act of Union' works as an allegory in which Ulster is the unruly child born as a result of the 'act of union' between 'imperially male' England and vulnerable and suffering Ireland. The poems in the second part of the book deal directly with the present, with blasted streets where 'the gelignite's a common sound effect', or with Heaney's own personal experiences in counterpoint with the events of the Troubles.

Heaney is a prolific writer and translator whose published verse since *North* includes *Field Work* (1979), *Station Island* (1984), *The Haw Lantern* (1987) and *Seeing Things* (1991). In 1995 – the year in which the peace process in Northern Ireland began in earnest – he was awarded the Nobel Prize for Literature. The committee commended Heaney for 'speaking out as an Irish Catholic about violence in Northern Ireland'.

Playwrights and politics

All kinds of writers, even those who may not have thought of themselves as 'political', were affected by the new political climate that had emerged at the end of the 1960s. Urban protests, particularly those of May 1968 in Paris, blurred the boundaries between theatre and protest: the streets themselves became the theatre. From this source a number of groups formed, and playwrights emerged who saw street theatre (or at least drama performed outside the confines of a conventional theatre) as the logical place for a radical challenge to political conservatism. It was not only the content of the plays that was oppositional, but also the method of production and location. The key dramatists emerging from this movement include Howard Brenton (1942-), David Edgar (1948-) and David Hare (1947-), who formed a theatre collective called David Hare's Portable Theatre. Another radical playwright, John McGrath (1935-2002), who had worked in cinema and television, set up a touring theatre company called 7:84; its title referred to the statistic that 7 per cent of the population owned 84 per cent of its wealth. At the same time women's liberation and gay rights organisations likewise began to challenge orthodoxy through theatrical performance. A notable example was the theatre collective Joint Stock, founded in 1975, who produced several plays by Caryl Churchill (1938-) among others.

Caryl Churchill was an established radio and stage playwright who had worked with another radical young company of women, Monstrous Regiment, on her play *Vinegar Tom* (1976), but it was the production, also in 1976, of her play about the English Revolution in the 17th century, *Light Shining in Buckinghamshire*, at the Royal Court (see page 18) that gave her work a higher profile. The play concerns the politics and religious conflicts of the English Civil War, in which individuals who are not seen as necessary by the politicians are destroyed. In *Cloud Nine* (1979) Churchill draws disconcerting parallels between colonial and sexual oppression. The first half of the play traces a 19th-century British colonial family where women are kept strictly in their place and the sexual double-standard is maintained, while the second half catapults the same characters forward in time to demonstrate, in a farcical way, the different sexual and gender freedoms in the late 20th century.

Alongside the new, young, theatre collectives, new plays by established writers such as Arnold Wesker (1932-), Harold Pinter, Tom Stoppard (1937-) and Edward Bond (1934-) were performed

— THE LIVING WORLD—

The 1970s was a decade of rapid technological and scientific advances which had a major impact on people's daily lives. It saw the introduction of the first domestic computers, initially in the form of pocket calculators, as well as the spread of colour television and video recorders. The world's first 'test tube' baby, Louise Brown, was born through in vitro fertilization (IVF) in England. The USA and Russia launched space probes to explore the solar system and even beyond. But many people were beginning to lose faith in technological progress because of its effect on the natural environment. For the first time there was an awareness that manmade pollution such as chlorofluorocarbons (CFCs) used in refrigerators and aerosol cans along with emissions from car and aeroplane engines, represented a serious threat to life systems on earth. Greenpeace was founded as an international organisation in 1971 to campaign against damage to the environment, and the following year the UN organised its first international summit conference on ecology.

Ecological issues are at the heart of one of the decade's most popular works of fiction, Watership Down *(1972) by Richard Adams (1920-). The novel, which was later made into both an animated film and a children's television series, is an odyssey of rabbits, whose adventures in search of a safe new settlement in the threatening world carry moral implications for human beings.*

---

in the commercial theatre in the 1970s. Tom Stoppard became famous through his play *Rosencrantz and Guildenstern Are Dead* (1966), which takes two minor characters from Shakespeare's *Hamlet* to create a world of bewildering meaninglessness. In addition to the obvious links with *Hamlet*, the play shares common features with Beckett's *Waiting for Godot* (see page 16); both plays are tragi-comedies whose central characters are lost and confused in a world which they do not understand and which seems hostile to them.

Stoppard is a 'political' writer, but not in an obvious way: his plays are playful rather than polemical. He uses satire, parody and verbal gymnastics to deal with serious philosophical and moral issues, playing with ideas and asking questions about the nature of illusion, reality and truth. In *Jumpers* (1972) a moral philosopher preparing a lecture on the existence of God, and on the related problem of the objectivity of good and evil, is confronted by the murder of an acrobat at a party in his own home. *Travesties* (1974) is a satire on English culture which includes characters from fiction, reality and history: James Joyce, Lenin, the Dadaist poet Tristan Tzara and the more obscure figure of Henry Carr, a minor consular official, who became embroiled in a quarrel with Joyce and earned himself a negative mention in Joyce's novel *Ulysses*. The play is set in Zurich, and takes as its starting point an amateur production of Oscar Wilde's *The Importance of Being Earnest,* but it is also set inside Henry Carr's imagination and memory, which goes back to World War I. In *Travesties*, Stoppard draws together cultural preoccupations of the early 1970s, in particular debates about the relationship between art and revolution.

Edward Bond is a more directly political playwright, a pacifist whose plays focus on issues he sees as morally vital to the future of society. One of his most famous plays, *Saved* (1965) is a portrayal of urban violence which contains a scene of a baby being stoned to death in its pram by a group of disaffected youngsters. It was originally banned by the Lord Chancellor, but the abolition of theatrical censorship in 1968 (see page 38) meant that Bond, like other playwrights, was able to tackle topical, political issues and take on institutions like the church or royalty without fear of

—THE NATIONAL THEATRE—

The National Theatre building on the South Bank, designed by architect Denys Lasdun, was opened by the Queen in October 1976. Britain's National Theatre Company had come into being in 1963 after a campaign lasting more than 60 years, and was initially housed at the Old Vic theatre in Waterloo Road, but now it finally had its own home. The new building, a concrete structure intended to resemble an ocean liner, extended the South Bank arts complex designed for the Festival of Britain in 1951. The theatre has three auditoria: the open-stage Olivier, the proscenium Lyttelton Theatre and the Cottesloe studio space. Although the first productions were Hamlet *in the Lyttelton and* Tamburlaine the Great *in the Olivier, the National was committed to presenting not only classics from the British and international repertoire, but also new and radical drama by playwrights outside the commercial mainstream of West End theatre, such as Howard Brenton.*

restriction. His subsequent plays written in the 1970s (*Lear,* 1971; *The Sea,* 1973; *Bingo,* 1974; *The Fool,* 1975) are all, in their different ways, representative of Bond's outspoken indictment of capitalist society. He symbolizes the importance of political choice through the dilemmas he sets up for his characters. *Lear,* for example, is a contemporary re-working of Shakespeare's *King Lear,* in which the character of Lear makes a political journey rather than the spiritual one of the original. The background to *Lear* is violent revolution; instead of accepting his lot at the end of the play like Shakespeare's protagonist, Bond's Lear has learned that he must accept responsibility for his life and take direct political action.

Howard Brenton is another radical playwright whose work, like that of Edward Bond, is preoccupied with violence as a moral as well as political issue. His epic play *The Romans In Britain* caused an uproar when it was first performed in 1980, particularly for a scene in which a Roman soldier attempts to rape a Druid boy. The play moves forward in time from BC to AD 1980, inviting comparison between imperialist domination in Roman Britain and that in contemporary Northern Ireland.

Television continued both to nurture its own writers, like Jack Rosenthal (*Bar Mitzvah Boy*, 1976) and the prolific Dennis Potter (*Pennies From Heaven*, 1978; *Blue Remembered Hills*, 1979) and to draw in writers from other media, for whom the experience was much less constricting than cinema work. Tom Stoppard and Michael Frayn (1933-) wrote original plays, and Kingsley Amis was happy to write episodes of the police series *Softly Softly*.

Turning away from liberation

The late 1970s was a time of revolution in the world, and Britain was not exempt. But many ordinary people felt that 'liberation' had gone too far. They wanted more order and authority, and they found it in Britain's first woman prime minister, Margaret Thatcher, who came to power in the general election of 1979. She headed a Conservative government dedicated to market forces and unfettered capitalism. In the early years the focus was on smashing the trade unions and slashing the budget: privatisation would come later. The old Labour government headed by James Callaghan slipped into oblivion, exhausted by economic crisis and internal dissent. Its last attempt at reform was the proposal to introduce devolved government in Scotland and Wales, provided that a referendum indicated decisive support. In Wales, the proposal was rejected; in Scotland, there was a narrow majority in favour, but too narrow to meet the criteria for going ahead. Taken together with the continuing unrest in Northern Ireland, this seemed symptomatic of Britain at the end of the decade: the United Kingdom was holding together, but not without considerable tensions.

5. THE 1980S: THE END OF CONSENSUS

Britain's first woman prime minister, Margaret Thatcher, was elected in 1979 and remained in power for the next 10 years. In the minds of many people, the 1980s are synonymous with Thatcherism, a loose concept encompassing the policies of Thatcher's government: strengthening the powers of central government, curbing the powers of trade unions and local government, and the active promotion of individualism and private enterprise. The Thatcher government was committed to privatisation in every area of life – including the arts as well as industry, welfare and education services. Its aim was to promote consumer culture and individualism: one of Margaret Thatcher's most famous remarks was 'there is no such thing as society, only individual men and women'.

Thatcherism is also identified with a strong tendency towards nationalism, which was particularly evident during the Falklands conflict. The distant British outpost of the Falkland Islands was invaded by its nearest neighbour, Argentina (who had long claimed the islands as the Malvinas) in April 1982. The response of the British government was immediate and forceful: Britain's two remaining aircraft carriers and dozens of other war vessels, many fighter planes and 10,000 troops were assembled in a task force and dispatched to the South Atlantic. In a swift and successful campaign the islands were recaptured and the Union Jack flew once again in Port Stanley on 14 June. The victory was largely symbolic: Britain may have lost its Empire, but it could still display its power and demonstrate its military, naval and technological superiority over a military dictatorship such as the Argentine republic.

National pride may have been temporarily revived over the Falklands, but many writers such as Harold Pinter (see page 31) were outspoken in opposing Thatcher's belligerence. On the domestic front there were still strikes, economic decline and social discontent in the early 1980s. The summer of 1981 had seen the worst riots of the century, with violent confrontations between black and white youths and the police in the Toxteth area of Liverpool and in Brixton in south London, among several other inner city areas.

Unemployment was particularly serious for young black people and there was a pervasive background of discrimination in jobs, housing and social opportunities. Violence and intimidation also played a part in some of the bitter and prolonged protests by trade unions in the early years of the decade. Mounted riot police were called in to disperse picketers during the coal miners' strike which began in 1984 and lasted a whole year. The miners' strike, which had begun in opposition to a programme of pit closures, proved

Miners' strike

The leader of the National Union of Miners, Arthur
Scargill (right of picture), leads a group of striking miners
in 1985. The strike, which started in 1984, lasted for a
year and ended with the eventual defeat of the strikers
by Margaret Thatcher's Conservative government.

that Thatcher was capable of systematically undermining trade union power. Coal was less essential to Britain's energy supplies than in the past, and in the end the National Union of Miners was defeated and many pits were closed for good. There were also peaceful protests, most notably at Greenham Common in Berkshire. In 1982 a group of women set up a peace camp outside Greenham Common air base to protest at the proposed siting there of American nuclear cruise missiles. Despite their efforts, which included blockading the base and cutting down parts of the fence, the first cruise missiles arrived in 1983, but the protests continued throughout the 1980s. Even after the missiles sited at Greenham were removed in 1991 the peace camp remained as a continuing protest against nuclear weapons. The last of the 'Greenham women' left the base in 2000.

All these problems were intensified by a government which seemed to be the most overtly right-wing that Britain had known in the 20th century. At the same time, the Labour Party – now under the leadership of CND supporter Michael Foot – appeared to be moving equally far to the left. In 1982 a new centrist political party, the Social Democrats, was formed by dissident right-wing members of the Labour Party, which subsequently formed an alliance with the Liberals; it included prominent figures such as the former Chancellor of the Exchequer Roy Jenkins, and for a brief period it seemed a genuine challenger to the two established parties. Despite this, the 1983 general election was a triumph for Thatcher and the Conservatives, who gained their largest majority since 1935. The result was a disaster for Labour, which was virtually wiped out in the south of England. The Thatcher government now began to implement a radical programme of privatisation and centralisation. Industries that had previously been owned by the state such as British Telecom, British Steel and British Gas were all privatised, in the belief that this would bring more competition, a better service and cheaper prices. Local government power was eroded by the abolition of some metropolitan councils, such as the Greater London Council in 1986, the control of local government expenditure through 'rate capping' and the introduction of the controversial community charge, or Poll Tax, in 1989.

The power of money

As industries became privatised, so share ownership became more widespread. There was a boom in consumer spending, and society appeared to be becoming more affluent, at least in parts of Britain. Where once the economy had depended on manufacturing industry, now it was centred on financial services, credit and investment. The most important example of government deregulation was that of the finance sector in 1986, known as the Big Bang, which opened trading to a wide range of financial institutions including foreign banks. The City was likened to an international casino, where many of the world's most astute – and highly paid – people competed for profits. The proliferation of bright young people earning six- and even seven-figure salaries gave rise to a new collective noun, 'Yuppies', an acronym version of the phrase 'Young Urban Professional'.

The ascendance of money and the yuppy culture in Thatcher's Britain is the subject of Caryl Churchill's satirical play, *Serious Money* (1987), a highly topical study of the effects of the Big Bang in the City. The traditional hierarchies of the stockbroking world with its entrenched class assumptions are threatened by brash young outsiders, who have been allowed onto the Stock Exchange as a result of deregulation. The play's rapid pace and structure, with its dizzying flashbacks and forwards and occasional eruption into rhyming couplets, echo the confused conditions of the new financial 'melting pot'. One of the play's characters, Zac, sums up the situation in a few lines:

> The British Empire was a cartel.
> England could buy whatever it wanted cheap
> and make a profit on what it made to sell.
> The Empire's gone but the City of London keeps
> on running like a cartoon cat off a cliff – bang.
> That's your Big Bang.
> End of City cartel.
> Swell.

Churchill's earlier play, *Top Girls* (1982) is also directly concerned with Thatcherism, exploring the superficial 'liberation' of women in the early 1980s. It contrasts the lifestyles and beliefs of two sisters at opposing ends of the spectrum. Marlene has fought her way to the top job in an advertising agency, and (like Margaret Thatcher herself) is a woman in a man's world who has elbowed a few men out of the way in her quest for power. Not surprisingly, she is a supporter of Margaret Thatcher and her monetarist economic policies. Her sister, Joyce, lives in the country, is a stay-at-home mother and believes in communal values rather than individualism. The argument between the sisters is not resolved, and the choice each has made seems to be equally valid in its own terms.

The greedy and materialistic 1980s is the theme of a 1984 novel by Martin Amis (1949-), aptly titled *Money*, and subtitled *A Suicide Note*. Set in New York, its central 'character' is money, although there is a human narrator in the form of a yuppy film producer, John Self, whose appetite for drink, pornography and sex leads to his becoming overwhelmed by a series of catastrophes.

Amis uses characteristically flamboyant language to describe with
relish a dehumanised, junk-food civilisation. The narrative is an
exaggerated and comic version of modern life in which money, it
seems, has taken on a life of its own. Martin Amis introduces
himself as a minor character in the novel, and refers to his father,
Kingsley Amis (see page 21), who was openly critical of his son's
literary development. Amis's ability simultaneously to satirise and
wallow in the worst aspects of contemporary culture, to take delight
in disgusting details, and his fascination with the sex-obsessed male
psyche is also demonstrated in his earlier novels (*The Rachel
Papers*, 1973; *Dead Babies*, 1975; *Success*, 1978). Amis's heroes
are often the type of male that later came to be defined as 'the
new lad'; someone at ease with his own sexual interests and
unconcerned with politically correct feminism.

A divided nation

The economic policies of the Thatcher years resulted in certain
areas of Britain, particularly the Southeast and some parts of the
Midlands, becoming more affluent while others – including the
Southwest, northern England, Scotland and Wales – bore the brunt
of the 'leaner and meaner' measures through huge increases in
unemployment. The 'north-south divide' was not only evident in
house prices; it was also apparent in the literature that was being
produced in Britain in the 1980s.

Some of the most interesting and inventive fiction written during
the period came from a group of Scottish writers whose use of
dialect and vocabulary vividly expressed political as well as literary
dissent, contributing to a debate about national identity and what it
meant to be British. James Kelman (1946-) used the language of
the streets to write about the lives of working-class Glaswegians in
The Busconductor Hines (1984) and *A Disaffection* (1989), a
powerful portrayal of an alcoholic secondary-school teacher. Alasdair
Gray (1934-) used gothic fantasy underpinned with realism to
conjure up a harsh version of Glasgow in his epic *Lanark: A Life in
Four Books* (1981).

Another Glasgow-based writer, Liz Lochhead (1947-) used
Scottish speech idioms to bring alive her woman-centred plays and
poetry from the early 1970s onwards. Her work is often humorous
and satirical, aiming above all at accessibility. In the 'historical'
drama *Mary Queen of Scots Got Her Head Chopped Off* (1987)
Lochhead uses her customary techniques of alienation and
anachronism to problematise the idea of woman as victim. Class is
raised as an issue: the actors playing Mary and Elizabeth also play
the maid of the other, Bessie and Marian. Other plays include *True
Confessions* (1982), and an adaptation into Scots of Molière's
Tartuffe (1985), again full of anachronisms and speech from various

eras and areas. Lochhead's collections of poetry include *True Confessions and New Cliches* (1985), performance pieces with many examples of ironic humour about the position of heterosexual feminists in Britain in the 1970s and 1980s, caught between their sexuality and their politics. In *Bagpipe Muzak* (1991), Scotland, and Glasgow in particular, become the targets of Lochhead's satire. 'Bagpipe Muzak, Glasgow, 1990' parodies Glasgow's marketing as European City of Culture. The poem concludes by denouncing a Conservative government that Scotland did not elect:

> So – watch out Margaret Thatcher,
> and tak' tent Neil Kinnock
> Or we'll tak the United Kingdom and
> brekk it like a bannock.

Literature after consensus

The range of new voices that emerged in the novels of the 1980s demonstrated the end of literary, along with political, consensus. In formal terms, there was a shift – begun in the late '70s – from realism as the dominant mode to writing commonly termed as 'post-modern'. Post-modern thought claims that 'reality' is a construct of language and narration, rather than something that is actually there to be observed. In the novel, devices such as the questioning or foregrounding of the role or existence of the author, the relationship between fact and fiction, between the past and the present, and that between truth and narrative all serve to break down the idea of a 'real', observable world. Writers including Ian McEwan (1948-), Peter Ackroyd (1949-), Julian Barnes (1946-) and Graham Swift (1949-) as well as Martin Amis can loosely be described as writing fiction in a post-modern mode, although the extent to which they depart from a realist base varies greatly.

Ian McEwan's novels and short stories show a fascination for the more perverse side of human nature, as in his first two short story collections, *First Love, Last Rites* (1975) and *In Between the Sheets* (1977). In his macabre first novel, *The Cement Garden* (1978), incest is the theme as two brothers and two sisters avoid being split up after the death of their mother by burying her body in cement. McEwan is a storyteller whose notion of the evil in everyday

— **BOOKER PRIZEWINNERS**—
IN THE 1980S

The concept of literary prizes was not new, but it was in the 1980s that competitions such as the Booker Prize became newsworthy events and began to have a mediating influence on book publishing. It was originally open to citizens of the British Commonwealth and the Republics of South Africa and Ireland, but from 2002 is also open to authors from the USA.

1980: William Golding, Rites of Passage
1981: Salman Rushdie, Midnight's Children
1982: Thomas Keneally, Schindler's Ark
1983: J.M. Coetzee, Life and Times of Michael K
1984: Anita Brookner, Hotel du Lac
1985: Keri Hulme, The Bone People
1986: Kingsley Amis, The Old Devils
1987: Penelope Lively, Moon Tiger
1988: Peter Carey, Oscar and Lucinda
1989: Kazuo Ishiguro, The Remains of the Day

life underlies all his work. *The Child in Time* (1987) is Ian McEwan's most obviously 'political' novel, set in a drab, authoritarian version of Thatcher's Britain, which balances fantasy with realism. It has three main components: the attempt of Stephen Lewis, a writer of children's books to find his lost infant daughter and repair the relationship with his estranged wife; his membership of a government commission on childcare; and his dealings with a former government minister, once his publisher, who is regressing to a state of childhood. This last character is a parody of the rising Tory MP: 'I have my mandate – a freer City, more weapons, good private schools'. The major theme of the book, however, is time itself, looked at from the emotional and psychological responses of Stephen Lewis to the time-stopping event of the loss of his daughter. His recovery and eventual re-entry into the continuum of human time form the basis of the novel. McEwan was nominated for the Booker Prize several times and he finally won in 1998 with *Amsterdam*, a black comedy whose subject is deception, both of others and of self. *Atonement* (2001), is an ambitious and complex novel set in the 1930s and '40s, with many literary influences including Virginia Woolf, E.M. Forster and D.H. Lawrence.

Like McEwan, Julian Barnes experimented with form in a deliberate attempt to make something new of the novel in the 1980s. His first novel was *Metroland* (1981), set partly in contemporary suburban London and partly in Paris during the student protests of 1968. *Flaubert's Parrot* (1984) is a mixture of literary commentary, biographical detection and fictional self-analysis. Its hero is a middle-aged, divorced doctor who visits the French writer Flaubert's birthplace of Rouen in search of memorabilia. The novel is concerned with the state of art in the late 20th century, and confronts the question of whether society has come to the end of the era of culture. Barnes's other 1980s novels, each of which explores a different area of experience, include *Before She Met Me* (1982), *Staring At The Sun* (1986) and *A History of the World in 10½ Chapters* (1989). Graham Swift's 1983 novel, *Waterland*, combines fact and fiction to recover buried history. The novel is an evocation of the secret world of the East Anglian fen country. Its intricate narrative serves to show how there is no single 'history', but many different versions of the past, all of which have a bearing on contemporary experience. The mysterious waterland of the fens with its ever-shifting borders is also an image of human consciousness and identity. Peter Ackroyd is another writer who explores active relationships between the past and the present in his novels. In *Hawksmoor* (1985), a modern-day detective investigates a series of murders in London churches that become linked to the rebuilding of the city after the Great Fire of London, while in *Chatterton* (1987) modern events are linked back to the death of the poet Thomas Chatterton and the marriage of the Victorian writer George Meredith. Ackroyd is fond of recreating the past through its own language; half of *Hawksmoor* is written in an imitation 17th-century English to record the point of view of Nicholas Hawksmoor, the architect of the six great East End churches where the murders occur. Thomas Chatterton was himself a notorious imitator of the writing of other periods, making his name by writing fake medieval poetry, so lends himself as an obvious subject to Ackroyd's own talents in this area.

Poetic observations

Like their novelist counterparts, some contemporary poets were not directly concerned with politics, preferring to stand back and observe the society of the time from a distance. One of the best known poets of the 1980s is Craig Raine (1944-), whose style of bizarre, often unconnected metaphors was developed in his first two volumes of work, *The Onion, Memory* (1978) and *A Martian Sends A Postcard Home* (1979). Much of Raine's poetry exhibits a concern with family, particularly with the role of the father, and with a 'crisis of masculinity'. He and other poets, including Christopher Reid (1949-), were described as the 'Martian School' because of the way they specialised in imaginative similes, describing everyday objects in original ways to make them seem strange and alien – for example in these lines from 'A Martian Sends a Postcard Home':

> Only the young are allowed to suffer openly
> Adults go to a punishment room with water but nothing to eat.
> They lock the door and suffer the noises alone
> No one is exempt and everyone's pain has a different smell.

Raine continued with the same approach in *A Free Translation* (1981) and *Rich* (1984), in which his father appears in a central prose account of his childhood. One of his best known and most ambitious works is a 'novel' in verse, *History: The Home Movie* (1994), which chronicles his own family and that of the Pasternaks against a background of 20th-century European history.

Many poets, of course, were firmly committed to writing about the political and social dislocation evident during the Thatcher years. Tony Harrison (1937-) was among the most uncompromising of these: born and educated in Leeds with a degree in classics, he believes strongly in the power of public performance, and the theme of many of his poems is the legacy of class and power on culture. His long poem *v.* was made into a controversial television film, and takes as its starting point the graffiti sprayed on his parents' gravestone in a Leeds cemetery:

61

Vs sprayed on the run at such a lick,
the sprayer master of his flourished tool,
gets short-armed on the left like that red tick
they never marked his work with much at school.

Half this skinhead's age but with much approval,
I helped whitewash a V on a brick wall.
No one clamoured in the press for its removal
or thought the sign, in wartime, rude at all.

These Vs are all the versuses of life
from LEEDS v. DERBY, Black/White
and (as I've known to my cost) man v. wife,
Communist v. Fascist, Left v. Right,

class v. class as bitter as before,
the unending violence of US and THEM,
personified in 1984
by Coal Board MacGregor and the NUM.

The new literary 'establishment' did not, however, consist
entirely of male writers writing about society (or indeed masculinity)
in crisis. Rose Tremain (1943-) came to critical attention during
the decade with novels including *The Swimming Pool Season*
(1985) and *The Cupboard* (1989), as well as two collections of
short stories. *Restoration* (1989) is a historical novel written in the
first person, concerned with a student of anatomy at the court of
King Charles II. Tremain returned to the historical novel with *Music
& Silence* (1999), set in 17th-century Denmark. A.S. (Antonia)
Byatt (1936-) along with her sister, Margaret Drabble (see page
29), continued to be prominent and popular novelists. Byatt won
the Booker Prize for *Possession* (1990), the story of two 1980s
academics whose paths cross when they find that the two Victorian
poets they are researching were linked in a passionate love affair.
The novel is written in pastiches of 19th-century literary styles,
including letters, diaries and poetry. Anita Brookner (1928-) won
the Booker Prize for her novel *Hotel du Lac* (1984), in which a
romantic novelist takes refuge in a Swiss hotel out of season and
meets a man whom she thinks will transform her life. In the genre of
crime fiction, the two most popular and critically praised writers were
also women: P.D. (Phyllis) James (1920-) and Ruth Rendell
(1930-), who also began writing psychological thrillers under
the pseudonym of Barbara Vine in the 1980s.

Gay writing broke into the mainstream in the 1980s with
novelists such as Jeanette Winterson (1959-). Winterson's first,
and most critically acclaimed novel, was the semi-autobiographical

Oranges Are Not The Only Fruit (1985), a witty study of a provincial childhood passed within the narrow, women-dominated confines of an evangelical Christian sect. Her next novel, *The Passion* (1987) was also enthusiastically received. With the fantastic, quasi-historical *Sexing the Cherry*, (1989) Winterson moved into more experimental forms of writing. The feminist theory underpinning much of Winterson's fiction is that gender is a construct, rather than a given.

The wider world

Britain moved closer to Europe when, after nearly 200 years of false starts, Britain and France finally agreed to link their two countries with a pair of undersea rail tunnels in 1986. Margaret Thatcher and President François Mitterand made the historic announcement in Lille in 1986, and the first passengers made the trip through the Channel tunnel from Folkestone to Calais in 1994. But despite the gradual strengthening of links with Europe, Thatcher always remained publicly hostile to any form of integration.

Multicultural Britain began to be reflected in different ways in the literature and drama of the 1980s. A new generation of writers, including Chinese-born Timothy Mo (1950-) and Japanese-born Kazuo Ishiguro (1954-), as well as Salman Rushdie (1947-), brought a non-European cultural awareness to the sometimes narrow perspective of the English novel. In *Sour Sweet* (1983), Timothy Mo describes the closed, protective, alienated and opportunistic society of the London Chinese, while in his panoramic novel *An Insular Possession* (1986) he explores the beginnings of Hong Kong as a British trading colony following the 'Opium War' of 1839-42. In *The Remains of the Day* (1989) Kazuo Ishiguro asks demanding cultural questions about British society. The novel makes the life of a dutiful, sycophantic servant in a large country house synonymous with Britain's policy of appeasement towards the Germans in the 1930s.

Salman Rushdie is often classed as one of the exponents of magic realism (see Glossary of Terms). Born in Bombay to a Muslim family and educated in England, Rushdie came to literary prominence with *Midnight's Children* (1981), for which he won the Booker Prize. It tells the story of Saleem Sinai, who was born on the stroke of midnight on the day that India was granted independence and whose life becomes emblematic of the political and social destiny of the new generation. Rushdie was thrown into notoriety in 1989 when the Iranian leader Ayatollah Khomeini invoked a death sentence, or *fatwa*, upon him as a result of his epic novel *The Satanic Verses* (1988), which was explicitly critical of Islam. Its title refers to verses cut from the Koran by the Prophet as inspired by Satan; in one, prostitutes play out a fantasy that they are the Prophet's wives. The book was already banned in India and there had been protests in Britain by the time the *fatwa* was pronounced on Rushdie and on its publishers. Rushdie apologised, but his apology was rejected and he was forced to go into hiding under police protection. Defence of the book and of Rushdie's right to express his own point of view raised issues about censorship, freedom and the rise of religious fundamentalism in Britain in the late 1980s.

In the theatre, writers explored the idea of 'Britishness' from a variety of cultural perspectives. The playwright Mustapha Matura (1939-) founded the Black Theatre Co-operative in 1979, one of a number of ventures designed to raise the profile of West Indian experience in Britain. Matura's own plays include *Play Mas* (1974) and *The Coup* (1991). The black British writer Caryl Phillips (1958-) made displacement the subject of his 1982 play, *Where There is Darkness*. The father, Albert, is on the verge of returning to the West Indies and confronts his son with his own version of the black-British experience: 'Since you old enough to switch on your ears I done been telling you black people in this country must act and feel like a tribe or they not going to survive. But what fucking use is a tribe if nobody taking any notice of the elders them?'

Hanif Kureishi (1954-) is another British-born 'post-colonial' writer whose career was launched in the theatre; his early plays include *The Mother Country* and *Borderline*. Kureishi had also established a reputation as a screenwriter by the time his first novel, *The Buddha of Suburbia*, was published to great critical acclaim in 1990. The novel is an account of the tensions underlying multicultural Britain in the late 1980s. It tells the story of Karim Amir, a young man of Pakistani and English origin, who is trying to escape from the stifling boredom of suburban life into the wider world of 'real' London. Kureishi's next novel, *The Black Album* (1995), which was written as a response to *The Satanic Verses* affair, tackles the subject of Islamic fundamentalism and the sense of belonging among young British Asians.

'It's a funny old world'

These were Margaret Thatcher's words after she had been ousted as Conservative Party leader in 1990 and replaced by the more moderate John Major. Thatcherism had run into severe difficulties in the late 1980s, particularly over attempts to introduce market forces into the National Health Service. A proposal to abolish the system of household rates and replace it with the so-called Poll Tax (officially known as the community charge) led to widespread public protest and even rioting in several parts of Britain. At the same time, the apparent revival in the economy began to fade, and unemployment once again rose sharply. Thatcher's very personal and imperious style of leadership also lost credibility.

Good (1983)
Gilbert and George

Gilbert and George (1943- and 1942-) were among the most fashionable British artists of the 1980s. From the late 1960s onwards they developed new ways of showing taboo-breaking images of the social world, and, most notably, bodily fluids and waste. Their characteristic style is huge, brightly coloured photo-based collage pictures on a black grid.

6. TOWARDS THE MILLENNIUM

John Major became prime minister in 1990, after Margaret Thatcher was persuaded to resign by the growth of opposition even within her own party to her authoritarian style of leadership. Though his leadership would in turn be criticised in many quarters as weak, Major's administration was punctuated by a series of significant political initiatives. Within months of taking office he successfully steered the government through conflict in the Gulf where, in August 1990, Iraq under the leadership of Saddam Hussein invaded and annexed Kuwait. A coalition of 28 nations, led by the USA and including Britain, France and Egypt, embarked upon an air offensive known as 'Operation Desert Storm' that lasted six weeks. During a 100-hour ground war the 200,000-strong Iraqi army holding Kuwait was driven back.

Major's negotiations were also successful at the 1991 summit meeting of the European council in the Dutch town of Maastricht, where Britain was allowed to defer its decision on whether to join the single European currency, and to opt out of the proposed 'social chapter' of the treaty. By 1992 it looked as if Labour was about to come back to power, but the Conservatives won the general election with a comfortable majority, their fourth straight win. In December 1993 Major signed the Downing Street Declaration with the Irish Taoiseach, Albert Reynolds, committing Britain and Ireland to seeking a joint solution to the problem of Northern Ireland. But Major's administration is likely to be remembered at least as much for its failures, particularly the stock market crisis known as 'Black Wednesday' on 16 September 1992, when Britain was forced to pull out of the European Exchange Rate Mechanism.

Disillusion

By the mid-1990s there was much public disillusion with the state of British society in general, and with the Conservative administration in particular. An atmosphere of 'sleaze' surrounding politics was a major contributory factor to its decline. In 1992 the Heritage Secretary David Mellor resigned after revelations in the tabloid press of his affair with actress Antonia da Sancha, and this was followed by other sexual and financial scandals involving Conservative politicians, whose behaviour was felt to demonstrate the hypocrisy of a party which had proclaimed its attachment to 'family values'; Mellor had himself made prominent use of his own wife and children in his election publicity. A succession of court cases exposed the double standards of MP Neil Hamilton, former minister Jonathan Aitken, and former Deputy Chairman of the party Lord Archer, the latter two serving prison sentences for perjury. At the same time, many previously respected institutions were now under fire, including the monarchy, which found itself facing a wave of popular criticism.

When the Queen spoke publicly of her 40th anniversary year, 1992, as an 'annus horribilis', this was recognised as referring, among other things, to the continuing marital problems of her children, and to a fire that had devastated one of her residences, Windsor Castle. Rather than creating sympathy for her, the fire had caused resentment at the idea that public funds should be spent on the repairs, and she also had to heed pressure to pay a measure of income tax. The public hostility between the Prince and Princess of Wales intensified in 1995 when Diana admitted adultery during the course of a BBC TV interview, and referred to Charles's own adultery with Camilla Parker-Bowles, casting doubts on whether he would ever become king; the couple were divorced the following year.

Faith in the City of London was undermined by the sudden instability of the great insurance institution, Lloyd's of London, and by the Robert Maxwell scandal. After this flamboyant media tycoon, publisher of the *Daily Mirror*, died in mysterious circumstances in 1991 in a fall from his private yacht in the Mediterranean, it was discovered that he had dishonestly appropriated huge sums from the *Mirror*'s pension fund in order to shore up other failing companies. The inability of the City to enforce effective controls was further demonstrated when another scandal followed in 1995: Britain's oldest merchant bank, Baring's, failed to prevent a 'rogue trader', Nick Leeson, from running up a loss of $850 million in currency speculation in Hong Kong. The apparent licence given to the pursuit of wealth was typified by the accelerating rise in the salaries of company directors and executives, known as 'fat cats'. The criminal justice system, too, saw a decline in public respect during the decade. The release by the appeal court of the 'Birmingham Six', Irishmen imprisoned many years previously after the bombing of a Birmingham pub, was one of several such cases which exposed police injustice, and the Metropolitan Police were later found guilty, by a judicial report, of 'institutional racism' for the half-hearted way they investigated the murder of a black London youth, Stephen Lawrence, in 1993.

City life

The Canary Wharf and other modern housing developments in London's docklands contrasted starkly with the young homeless people sleeping rough in 'cardboard cities' around the capital. Disparities in wealth, income, health and lifestyle had grown ever wider. There was long-term youth unemployment in many parts of Britain, many troubled housing estates and an endemic drug culture in urban areas. The realities of city life were represented in literature in many different ways, particularly from the point of view of those on the margins. The disturbing novel *Trainspotting* (1993) by Irvine Welsh (1958-) documents the marginalised lives of a group of young people in a 'peripheral' Edinburgh housing scheme, whose motivation and identity are dominated by heroin. Welsh, like fellow Scottish writers James Kelman and Alasdair Gray (see page 58), used contemporary working-class dialect to bring the novel alive. *Trainspotting*, filmed in 1996, brought its author immediate critical and cult success. Like the novel, the film (directed by Danny Boyle) was bold in its rejection of social realism, incorporating surrealistic fantasy sequences within its fast-moving narrative.

Another successful writer whose novels focus on contemporary urban culture is Roddy Doyle (1958-). Doyle comes from Dublin, and the north Dublin suburb where he worked as a teacher for many years became the setting for his Barrytown trilogy of novels: *The Commitments* (1987), *The Snapper* (1990) and *The Van* (1991). In these three books, Doyle evokes a bleak modern cityscape as distinctive as the literary landscape of other Irish writers such as Joyce or Yeats. The Barrytown novels are dominated by dialogue, rather than description or inner thoughts. The language is funny and loud, full of slang and cursing. The trilogy focuses on the Rabbitts, a family of eight living on a housing estate whose lives are a mixture of domestic chaos and depressing poverty. *The Commitments* is about a group of Dubliners intent on forming a band, whose lives are far more influenced by American music and culture than by traditional Irish values. *The Van* celebrates the football fever that swept Dublin during the Italia '90 World Cup finals. All three novels were filmed soon after publication by leading English directors: *The Commitments* by Alan Parker, the other two by Stephen Frears. Doyle won the Booker Prize for his comic novel *Paddy Clarke Ha Ha Ha* (1993), a sensitive portrayal of the break-up of a marriage seen through the eyes – and written with the vocabulary and language structures – of a ten-year-old boy.

A different 'take' on city life is offered by Guyana-born writer Mike Phillips (1942-), who came to Britain in 1956. After school and a series of low-paid manual jobs, he started and lived in a hostel for homeless black youths in Notting Hill, leaving it to become a community activist in Manchester and Birmingham. He went into journalism in the 1970s and also began to write fiction, including a series of crime novels whose hero is Sam Dean, a London-based black British investigative journalist with a life in both black and white communities. The Sam Dean novels, which include *Blood Rights* (1989), *Point of Darkness* (1994) and *An Image to Die For* (1995), explore racial tensions in contemporary London. In his (non-fiction) book *Windrush* (1998), written to accompany a BBC TV series of the same name, Phillips chronicled the story of how West Indian immigration changed the face of British life during the 20th century.

Women in the 1990s

As the 21st century approached, women continued to make progress towards full equality. Ireland got its first woman president, Mary Robinson, in 1990. Her role was arguably more inspirational for other women – both in Ireland and beyond – than that of Mrs Thatcher, since she represented different, less aggressively 'masculine' values. In 1994 a long history of discrimination was ended when the first women priests in the history of the Church of England were ordained in Bristol Cathedral; although a minority have continued to oppose this reform, their influence has dwindled, and support is growing for the future appointment of women bishops.

Unlike the church, the novel had of course been the domain of women as much as men ever since the time of Jane Austen. The main new development at the end of the century was the genre of 'chick lit': brash, aggressively marketed novels by, and about, young women. The pioneer was *Bridget's Jones's Diary* (1997) by Helen Fielding: first a newspaper column, then a best-selling novel, then a successful film. Chick lit celebrated female angst, the single girl in the city who gets drunk with her girlfriends before meeting Mr Right, written in a witty, confessional form. Heroines like Bridget Jones represented the 'post-feminist' young woman in contemporary society, for whom issue-based feminism is a thing of the past, replaced by a readiness to go with the flow of consumerism, and to be 'one of the lads'.

Meanwhile, however, long-established women novelists like Margaret Drabble, her sister A.S. Byatt, and Fay Weldon (see page 45) continued to publish and to get serious critical attention. After her 26th novel *Jackson's Dilemma* (1995), Iris Murdoch's career was ended by Alzheimer's disease; her last years were chronicled by her husband John Bayley, and his best-selling memoir *Iris* was adapted into a successful film starring Judi Dench. A writer who came into her own in the 1990s was Pat Barker (1943-). Brought up in the northeast of England, Barker was encouraged to start writing after attending a creative writing course led by Angela Carter (see page 44). Her early novels, written in the tradition of working-class realism, are concerned with the lives of women, particularly women as survivors. Their world is one of poverty, of down-at-heel pubs, wastelands and violent men. Her first novel, *Union Street* (1982), is set in a depressed industrial north, creating seven portraits of women who are fighting to control their lives in an atmosphere of desperate poverty. *The Century's Daughter* (1986) tells the story of a woman who wants to save her community from disintegrating in the name of progress. Having survived a war and raised her children alone, she is determined not to give up.

Regeneration (1991), which begins a trilogy of novels on World War I, is different from Barker's earlier novels in many ways. It is set in the past, rather than the present; its location is mainly Scotland; its characters are nearly all men – British Army officers, some of them real historical figures – and its central subject is the theme of war and manhood. It follows the decorated officer and poet Siegfried Sassoon (1886-1967), who encounters the psychologist Dr Rivers (also a real person) during his treatment for shell-shock. Rivers is shown as a sympathetic but down-to-earth character, exhausted by the struggle of trying to deal with the horrors which confront him daily in the form of the traumatised men who come to him for treatment. *The Eye in the Door* (1993) features characters already encountered in the previous novel. Billy Prior, a former patient of Dr Rivers, is beginning to suffer from fugue states – episodes of which he has no memory. Through him the novel tells of the treatment of conscientious objectors at the time. In *The Ghost Road* (1995), which won the Booker Prize, Billy Prior's 'insanity' – or unwillingness to return to the killing fields – has supposedly been cured, and he must return to the front. In writing the trilogy, Barker asks searching questions posed by World War I: how many of its ghosts, and what long-term poisons from it are still at work inside us? As is evident from the work of Sassoon and his fellow war poet Wilfred Owen (1893-1918), war is terrible and to be avoided at all costs, but at the same time the experiences derived from it have a significant if unquantifiable value.

Since the 1980s, women's poetry, like women's fiction, has begun to deal with everyday female experience: food, work, leisure, consumerism, fashion, the family, socialising and sex alongside deeper issues. One of the most popular contemporary poets is Scottish-born Carol Ann Duffy (1955-) who, in 1999, was widely regarded as a leading contender for the new role of Poet Laureate following the death of the previous incumbent, Ted Hughes. Her first collection, *Standing Female Nude* (1985) was radical for the way the poems recorded female experience, often speaking what previously had been unspeakable in poetry from a female point of view. The title poem is a witty debunking of the myth of the male artist and his muse, spoken by the model:

> Six hours like this for a few francs.
> Belly nipple arse in the window light,
> he drains the colour from me. Further to the right,
> Madame. And do try to be still.
> I shall be represented analytically and hung
> In great museums.

Duffy can use imagery in a wholly anti-romantic way, while nevertheless creating a powerful sense of mood and occasion, as in 'Valentine' from *Mean Time* (1993):

I give you an onion.
Its fierce kiss will stay on your lips,
possessive and faithful
as we are.

Take it.
Its platinum loops shrink to a
wedding-ring,
if you like.

Duffy explores identity both personal and related to place, in poems about mothers and daughters, childhood and memory. Her poems tend to avoid sentimentality and to portray British society in contemporary, rather than idealised or nostalgic, versions. She writes about the uncomfortable social issues in Britain: racial tension, child neglect, youth unemployment and drug addiction. Much of her poetry also looks beyond her own experience to consider the position of ethnic minorities – as in 'Girl Talking', whose speaker is a young Muslim girl, 'Foreign' from *Selling Manhattan* (1987) and 'Originally' from *The Other Country* (1990). Duffy is also highly regarded for her many love (and hate) poems. Her most recent collection is *The World's Wife* (1999).

At the turn of the century, one of the most critically acclaimed novels was *White Teeth* (2000) by the young, half-Jamaican writer Zadie Smith (1976-), a raucous but also serious look at modern life in London. It spans 25 years of two families' assimilation in Willesden, north London; the Iqbals from Bangladesh and the Joneses from Jamaica. Their intertwined destinies distil the history and hopes of the British Empire in a multi-layered and detailed saga whose characters also include Jehovah's Witnesses, halal butchers, animal-rights activists and a group of Muslim militants.

Another fresh new female voice is that of the Scottish writer

— THE NATIONAL LOTTERY —

The National Lottery, an idea proposed from time to time in the past, became a reality in 1994. Publicity given to big winners sustained its popularity, and it has produced a steady stream of profits for investment in recreation and the arts. The most spectacular result has been the development of new public buildings or the improvement of existing ones such as sports centres, libraries, art galleries and museums in different parts of the UK. The impact on literature and theatre has been less notable, but the Irish poet and critic Tom Paulin is among the writers who have gained Lottery support for specific projects: he was awarded £75,000 to finance his research for an ambitious epic poem on 20th-century history, published in 2002 as The Invasion Handbook. *Large sums were also given to British film companies — but this was money simply for production, and there was no intervention in an exhibition system dominated by Multiplex cinemas and Hollywood films, so there was no guarantee that the films would actually be shown. Ironically, the lottery support was in many cases counter-productive, leading to an accumulation of films which piled up on the shelf, seen by few if any audiences, and tending to lower rather then raise the prestige of British cinema.*

A.L. (Alison) Kennedy (1965-), whose first collection of short stories was *Night Geometry and the Garscadden Trains* (1990). She was selected as one of the 20 best young British novelists in 1993 after the publication of her first novel, *Looking for the Possible Dance*. Another novel, *So I Am Glad* (1995), is a combination of satire, allegory and love story. Her third novel, *Everything You Need*, was published in 1999. Kate Atkinson (1951-) won the Whitbread book of the year award in 1995 for her first novel, *Behind the Scenes at the Museum*. It was followed by the equally successful and quirky *Human Croquet* (1997), set in England in the mid-1960s, which tells the story of a once-grand family, the Fairfaxes, who are now reduced to being the local grocers. Her third novel, *Emotionally Weird*, was published in 1999.

Despite the failure of so many lottery-funded films (see page 71), and the lack of a regular outlet for its product, British cinema continued to have intermittent success at both popular and prestige levels. Veteran directors Ken Loach and Mike Leigh were by now respected figures at Cannes and other festivals. *The Full Monty* (1997) and *Billy Elliot* (2000) updated the familiar pattern of the 'northern' film, dramatising the struggle against financial and spiritual deprivation in urban settings now transformed by the loss of their traditional industries. Offsetting this were more upmarket London-based films like *Four Weddings and a Funeral* (1994) and *Notting Hill* (1999), and the continuation of the 'heritage' genre in films that exploited English literature (for example, the adaptation of Jane Austen's *Sense and Sensibility* in 1993, scripted by its star Emma Thompson in a feminist spirit); and English history (*Elizabeth* in 1998, with Cate Blanchett as the Queen); and both at once in *Shakespeare in Love* (1998), scripted by Tom Stoppard. Meanwhile, a lively series of 'multicultural' films both reflected and celebrated a new mix in British society. The comedies *East is East* (1999) and *Bend it like Beckham* (2002), whose protagonists were from Asian immigrant families, were successfully marketed to general audiences, without being aimed, as they would have been in the USA, at a specific 'ethnic' market.

— SHAKESPEARE'S GLOBE—

A £30 million recreation of Shakespeare's Globe Theatre, built on London's Bankside overlooking the River Thames, admitted its first paying audience in 1996 and was officially opened by the Queen the following year. Built according to authentic Elizabethan practices, the 20-sided building has a thatched roof and open-air yard where some of the audience stand to watch plays, like the 'groundlings' of Shakespeare's day. Authenticity also applies to the way plays are produced at the Globe: there is no stage lighting or scenery, and few props. Shakespeare's Globe is only 200 metres from the site of the original, which was built by the Burbage brothers, who went into partnership with Shakespeare and his fellow actors in 1599 to fund the project. The new Globe's construction came about as a result of decades of campaigning and fundraising by the American actor Sam Wanamaker, who died in 1993 after work on the theatre had started, but before his dream had become a reality. The project has been carried on as Wanamaker wished by its actor-manager Mark Rylance. The first play to be staged at the Globe was The Two Gentlemen of Verona, *and since then productions have included many of Shakespeare's plays as well as contemporary works — just as was the case at the original Globe.*

———————

Four Weddings and a Funeral **(1994)**
Directed by Mike Newell
Starring Andie MacDowell (fourth from the left) and
Hugh Grant (second from the right), this British
romantic comedy was a huge international box
office success. It appeared to mark a revival in the
fortunes of British cinema in the mid-1990s, and
was part of the 'Cool Britannia' phenomenon.

New Labour and Cool Britannia

In May 1997, Labour at last returned to power, and by a huge majority. Its victory was due to a combination of Conservative demoralisation and its own rebranding as 'New Labour', consciously turning its back on socialist principles, such as nationalisation, which risked unpopularity. New Labour had a new leader in Tony Blair, who at the age of 43 became the youngest prime minister since 1812. Blair hailed the election victory as 'a vote for the future' and declared that 'we can put behind us the battles of the past century and address the challenges of the new century'.

In the same year, an exhibition appropriately named *Sensation*, which showcased Britain's leading younger artists, opened at the Royal Academy. The exhibition was put together from the Saatchi collection, and included work by one of Britain's most prominent artists of the late 20th century, Damien Hirst. His work *The Physical Impossibility of Death in the Mind of Someone Living* was a giant fish tank filled by a tiger shark floating in formaldehyde solution. Another of Hirst's works, *Mother and Child, Divided* – two sheep also pickled in a tank of formaldehyde – had won the Turner Prize two years earlier. The media and public interest in the exhibition, which attracted widespread publicity and scandal, appeared to suggest a new beginning, with Britain at the 'hip' heart of culture just as it had been in the 1960s. The phrase 'Cool Britannia' was coined in the American magazine *Newsweek* near the end of 1996, and began to appear in the British press shortly afterwards. Its icons were Princess Diana, who had become possibly the most famous and most glamorous person in the world, Britpop bands such as Oasis and Blur as well as The Spice Girls, footballers such as David Beckham, films including *Trainspotting* and *The Full Monty*, and even Tony Blair himself. Princess Diana died in a car crash in September 1997, releasing a huge and unprecedented wave of public emotion. After the initial outburst of grief the period of mourning was relatively short-lived, however, just like the phenomenon of 'Cool Britannia', which in essence was anti-modern or post-modern pastiche, rather than a genuine revival of 1960s anti-establishment energy and radicalism. Britpop songs such as Blur's 'Park Life' conjured up images of long-gone working-class community, while Oasis borrowed directly from the Beatles.

Political events that followed the May election seemed to reinforce this feeling of radical change. In June, one of the last traces of the British empire vanished as Hong Kong was returned to Chinese control after 155 years as a British colony. The hand-over had, of course, had been prepared long in advance, but Labour carried out its own new programme of constitutional reforms nearer to home. Some legislative power was devolved to Scotland and Wales in 1999, with the creation of representative parliamentary assemblies for both countries. In the same year, new efforts to break the political deadlock in Northern Ireland produced the Good Friday Agreement: the Irish Republic withdrew its territorial claim to the North, and arrangements were made for the transfer of significant powers back from Westminster to the Northern Ireland Assembly at Stormont. After lengthy and often bitter negotiations about the decommissioning of weapons held by paramilitary groups, the Assembly began operating in November 1999, though it was soon suspended, before being restored once more. Reform of the unelected House of Lords was begun in the same year, with a severe restriction on the power of the hereditary peers.

Despite this, there were many aspects of New Labour's policies that were similar to those of the Conservatives, and Blair firmly rejected any return to the traditional socialist values of 'old' Labour. Railway privatisation was one of many Conservative measures which Labour had fought against while in opposition, and promised to reverse, only to acquiesce in after its election. There was a policy of friendship towards business, and a corresponding weakening of the historic links with the trade union movement; charges were introduced for university tuition. Even the contrast with Conservative 'sleaze', which Labour had emphasised so successfully, was blurred by a series of dubious episodes which culminated in the resignation of one of Blair's closest political allies, Peter Mandelson. None of this seemed to affect the government's popular standing, and Labour was re-elected in 2001, again with a large majority in parliament. Labour had convincingly reinvented itself as a party of the centre right, and the Conservatives were still struggling to present a meaningful alternative.

Football culture, new lads and literature

Perhaps the most spectacular symbol of the changes of this period – and of the changes in British culture since 1945 – was the 'people's game' of football. In the post-war years, it was still mainly a game for working-class players and spectators. Wages were kept low, teams were all-British, and the most important international games were the annual encounters between England and Scotland. Even when British clubs began to play in Europe, and England won the World Cup in 1966, the framework did not radically change. But by 2002, football stars like David Beckham were earning more in one week than most other people earn in a full year. The main instrument of change was the setting up of an elite 'Premier League' in 1992, run independently of the lower divisions; its aim was to maximise the income available from television, and especially from the new satellite broadcasting channels. This access of wealth enabled the top clubs to pay high wages and to attract stars from overseas: the rise in glamour and skill attracted a new, wealthier following, without losing popular support. The football world became a theatre of conspicuous consumption led by Beckham and his wife, the former Spice Girl Victoria Adams, who are as celebrated as royalty. Significantly, Tony Blair took care to associate himself with the game, in contrast to John Major's well-publicised allegiance to cricket.

The cultural status of football was reinforced by a best-selling book about the game by fanatical Arsenal supporter Nick Hornby (1958-), *Fever Pitch*, published, significantly, in the same year (1992) that the Premiership began. After another book on football, *My Favourite Year* (1993), Hornby produced two novels – *High Fidelity* (1995) and *About a Boy* (1998). Like *Fever Pitch*, they were best-sellers, and were quickly adapted for cinema. Between them, these books complement *Bridget Jones* and the 'chick lit' genre (see page 69) in the way they dramatise, intensely but with a distancing irony, a set of laddish obsessions and anxieties. Hornby has commented that 'Nothing happens in the books... I'm creating a person who's a lot like the person reading the books.'

Alongside the rise of consumerism and branding, bolder forms of innovatory fiction have continued to be produced and, sometimes, to attract a wider readership. The phenomenal success of *Captain Corelli's Mandolin* (1994) by Louis de Bernières (1954-) is testament to this. Set on the Greek island of Cephalonia during World War II, the book demonstrates the way in which contemporary British novelists have become adept at using once-foreign modes of writing, while maintaining a realist base: de Bernières was influenced by the magic realism of the Colombian writer Gabriel García Márquez (1928-), in particular, but also by the English and European 'picaresque' (see Glossary of Terms) novel. Equally ambitious in its range and style is another novel of 1994, *What a Carve Up* by Jonathan Coe (1961-). The title refers both to a British comedy horror film of 1962 with which the narrator is obsessed, and to the 'carve-up' of British institutions and values, in the 1980s, by the Winshaws, a ruthlessly entrepreneurial family who take to a gruesome extreme the principles of Thatcherism: the interplay between these two frameworks gives the novel a savage comic energy. Ground-breaking in a different way is the work of the Indian-born novelist Vikram Seth (1952-), whose *A Suitable Boy* (1993), a massive saga of post-war Indian life, has a Dickensian scope, and, like *Captain Corelli*, reached an unexpectedly wide audience.

After the death of Ted Hughes in 1998 there was much discussion about whether the post of Poet Laureate was an embarrassing anachronism which should simply be abolished, or whether it could become relevant to contemporary Britain through

the appointment of a 'people's poet'. In the event, Andrew Motion
(1952-) was appointed. He was regarded by many critics as a safe
choice; a New Labour supporter who was in tune with contemporary
society, a champion of poetry and its continuing relevance, but not
as radical in his views or modes of expression as, say, Carol Ann
Duffy (see page 70) – and, crucially, a monarchist. Motion has
published eight collections of poetry and a *Selected Poems 1976-
1997*, as well as biographies of other poets including Keats and
Philip Larkin. In Motion's poetry the public and the personal are
closely entwined; he writes about his own family and friends
alongside historical and legendary figures. *Love in a Life* (1991) is a
narrative in which the stories of two marriages gradually emerge and
are brought together.

Children's literature?

One of the most widely noted developments in recent years has
been the trend for fantasy fiction written primarily for young
people to become immensely popular with adult readers. Some
commentators see this as yet another example of the 'dumbing
down' of literary culture, while others have identified a demand for
old-fashioned 'well-made' novels which – unlike much contemporary
fiction – acknowledge the importance of plot, rather than relying on
description and dialogue.

There can be few people in the Western world who have not
heard of the boy wizard Harry Potter, the creation of J.K. (Joanne
Kathleen) Rowling, (1966-). The first book in a projected series of
seven, *Harry Potter and the Philosopher's Stone*, was published in
1997, and the fourth in the series, *Harry Potter and the Goblet of
Fire* broke all publishing records when it went on sale in 2000 by
selling 372,775 copies on its first day. In an age dominated by
computer games and television, J.K. Rowling was credited with
getting children reading again, but so enthusiastic was the response
of adults that the books were also published in 'adult' versions with
different covers. Critics have praised Rowling's linguistic inventiveness,
comic timing and page-turning plots. The underlying themes of
friendship and loyalty established in the first two books are
developed into darker themes of betrayal, despair and bereavement
by the third book, *Harry Potter and the Prisoner of Azkaban* (1999).
Much more radical and subversive in its message is the *His Dark
Materials* trilogy – *Northern Lights* (1995), *The Subtle Knife* (1997)
and *The Amber Spyglass* (1999) – by Philip Pullman (1946-). The
series, a single story told in three volumes, was inspired by John
Milton's poem *Paradise Lost*, but in Pullman's version man's
temptation and fall are not the source of all human misery but the
end of repression by what he calls 'the Authority' – the institution of
the Church and formalised religion – and the beginning of liberation

and freedom of thought. In *The Amber Spyglass* (2000), it is two children whose knowledge saves the world, overturning the traditional idea of childhood innocence.

Literature in the 21st century

Inevitably, the start of a new millennium has prompted discussion of the evolving role of literature and the arts in a rapidly changing world. Politically, a major transforming event occurred on the morning of 11 September 2001, when two passenger jets crashed in quick succession into the twin towers of the World Trade Centre in New York, symbols of American power. Both towers soon collapsed into rubble, and more than 3000 people died. A third plane crashed into the Pentagon in Washington, causing several hundred more deaths; the destructive mission of a fourth was only narrowly foiled by action from passengers who forced it to crash prematurely. All four had been hi-jacked by Islamic militants; it was assumed, and soon confirmed, that their plans were co-ordinated by the Al-Qaida organisation, headed by the Syrian-born Osama Bin Laden. Television pictures of the attack and its aftermath were played and replayed around the world, creating outrage and, in a few countries, exultation. The United States gained immediate and wide support for its declaration of a 'war on terrorism', and for its aim of tracking down Bin Laden and punishing those who aided him; Tony Blair was especially forthright in underwriting the policies of President Bush. Not surprisingly, a global consensus was hard to maintain. Despite a successful campaign to oust the hard-line Taliban government in Afghanistan, Bin Laden was not found, and Bush's vision of a world divided between bad countries (an 'axis of evil') and good (including some dubious pro-US regimes) was increasingly seen as not just simplistic, but dangerous. Indirectly, the events of 11 September, or 9/11 as it is known in the US, have led to a dramatic increase in tension in other trouble spots.

As of 2002, it is hard to predict what the long-term effects of these upheavals will be, on the world or on literature. Ian McEwan,

— THE MILLENNIUM DOME—

In the mid-1990s the Conservative government under John Major decided Britain should have a spectacular exhibition to celebrate the millennium, just as the Festival of Britain had celebrated the arrival of a new, post-war age (see page 14). When the Labour Party was elected in 1997 it took the project on. Plans were drawn up for a giant Millennium Dome in Greenwich, southeast London; essentially a giant tent housing various exhibition zones including a Mind Zone, a Faith Zone and a Learning Zone. The Dome, which cost £780 million to build, was intended to be (in the words of Tony Blair) 'a great British achievement', but it was never entirely clear whether it was primarily intended to be a theme park-style entertainment, an educational experience, or a focus of national pride. When the Dome opened on New Year's Eve 1999 the initial response was lukewarm, and ticket sales — which had to meet a break-even target of 12 million visitors in the year the Dome was open — were disappointing. For many people, the Dome seemed to represent the confusion at the heart of late 20th-century British society, and its reception was very different from the response of the British public, and media, to the Festival of 50 years earlier. After the exhibition closed at the end of 2000, there was much debate about how best to use the Dome's tent-like shell. Eventually it was written off, and was given away to property developers two years later.

Tate Modern
Architects Jacques Herzog and Pierre de Meuron

Tate Modern is housed in the old Bankside Power Station, designed by Sir Giles Gilbert Scott and built between 1947 and 1963. Work began to transform the old power station into a new showcase for modern art in 1995, and the gallery finally opened in May 2000. A 10-m high 'spider' (above) by sculptor Louise Bourgeois was one of the opening exhibits in the Tate's huge Turbine Hall.

writing in *The Guardian* newspaper, was one of several novelists whose immediate journalistic response to the images from New York was heartfelt and eloquent. Subsequently, the playwright Harold Pinter was one of many intellectuals to protest against the whole concept of the 'war on terrorism', seeing American imperialism as the root cause of global instability. Significantly, it was a literary journal, the *London Review of Books*, that became, controversially, a main forum for this kind of criticism of American policy. In theatre, the Edinburgh festival fringe of 2002 was dominated by shows inspired by 9/11; they included *Project 9/11*, by the New York University's Playwright Horizon theatre, which relates seven personal accounts of living in New York on the day of the attack; a one-man show from the political satirist Michael Moore; and a controversial work on media reaction to the events by a drag queen, Tina C. Hollywood's immediate response was to withdraw, for reasons of taste, any films that might evoke 9/11 – even skyline shots with the twin towers were cut out – but this policy could not last. Undoubtedly, cinema, like all other arts and media, in America, Britain and elsewhere, will continue to reflect on the meaning of these events in complex and conflicting ways.

But this is only one aspect of the growing domination of British life by American events, influence and example. It is not only that every town has its MacDonalds restaurant and its Starbucks coffee house, often several of them, and a cinema dominated by American product. Publishers and television companies have increasingly been absorbed into a smaller number of large groupings, at the expense of regional and other diversities. Two symptomatic events of 2002 were the government's lifting of controls on the ownership of ITV stations, potentially opening them up to American control, and the proposal to make American novelists eligible for the Booker Prize, whose whole purpose had been to reward the achievement of British and Commonwealth writers.

Against this can be set the pull of another international influence: that of Europe. Inexorably, Britain has become politically further integrated year by year into the European community, and all the signs are that, having accepted a redesigned EC passport, public opinion is already prepared for Britain to join the common European currency, the Euro, launched in most other member countries at the start of 2002. At the same time, the Queen's Golden Jubilee celebrations in 2002 were, to the surprise of many, accompanied by a good-humoured patriotism. Friendly and unthreatening patriotism was also displayed at the football World Cup in Japan and Korea, where England reached the quarter finals.

The World Cup experience, shared simultaneously by people all over the globe, was made possible by an opening-up of communications which would have been unimaginable 50 years earlier. Another instance of this is of course the Internet, or World Wide Web. These developments have implications for literature and other media which are only beginning to be realised. The Internet has already taken over some of the functions of the newspaper, the reference library and the bookshop: at present there is a state of uneasy mutual support, but in the longer term the Internet may make more serious inroads. The Internet also offers opportunities to the publisher, resulting in on-line journals and even on-line books, pioneered by authors such as the American horror novelist Stephen King. On the one hand, this represents a means of 'democratising' and liberating literature: anyone can publish their writing on the Internet, without the need of an agent, a publisher, or, indeed, any funds, and there are few outside controls. On the other, its effect on conventional marketing may be to increase the concentration of more and more power in the hands of the big publishers and bookshop chains, as smaller operators are squeezed out.

Perhaps the most hopeful prediction is that the book as we know it, an undeniably convenient vehicle for the storage and retrieval of words, will continue to exist as part of a complex web of media possibilities. The cinema release of major films is now only part of an elaborate operation that encompasses the renting and sale of videos and DVDs, documentaries about the production, books of the film, special websites and other profitable spin-offs. Something comparable is already happening with the promotion of books; novels, from *Bridget Jones* to *Harry Potter*, have been rapidly processed for cinema, and given all the promotional trimmings. But the cinema experience is still at the heart of the operation, and indispensable to it, and the same is likely to be true of the book.

Meanwhile, novelists themselves contribute to the debate about the future of their medium. Jeanette Winterson (see page 62), whose novel *The Powerbook* (2000) features a gender-ambiguous e-writer and encompasses London, Paris and cyberspace, has stated that 'creative people must get involved with the Internet... For an artist it is another chance at communication.'

In David Lodge's *Thinks...* (2001), the female protagonist, Helen Read, is a novelist who teaches in that key institution for late 20th-century literature, the creative writing programme. In the course of the book she is taught for the first time to use e-mail, and sections of the novel consist of her e-mail exchanges. The male protagonist, Ralph Messenger, works in computing and artificial intelligence, and their personal relationship is intertwined with a professional one, as they debate the different forms of communication and consciousness in the light of contemporary research. 'I've always assumed, I suppose, that consciousness was the province of the arts, especially literature, and most especially the novel'; Helen's assumption is not defeated, but adapted within a new context.

TIMELINE

Science, technology and the arts	Literature	History
	1945 Orwell, *Animal Farm*; Waugh, *Brideshead Revisited*; Mitford, *The Pursuit of Love*	**1946** United Nations holds its first General Assembly
1946 First electronic computer built in USA	**1946** Rattigan, *The Winslow Boy*; Peake, *Titus Groan*	**1947** India and Pakistan become independent
1947 Britain's first atomic reactor at Hartwell starts up; launch of Edinburgh Festival	**1947** Lowry, *Under the Volcano*	**1948** National Health Service begins; State of Israel comes into existence
	1948 Greene, *The Heart of the Matter*; Fry, *The Lady's Not For Burning*	**1949** Eire leaves the Commonwealth, becoming the Republic of Ireland
	1949 Orwell, *Nineteen Eighty-four*; Bowen, *The Heat of the Day*; Eliot, *The Cocktail Party*	**1950** Korean War begins
1951 Festival of Britain	**1951** Powell, *A Question of Upbringing* (first volume of *A Dance to the Music of Time*)	**1952** Mau-Mau rebellion in Kenya
1952 First British atom bomb exploded; *The Mousetrap* opens in London	**1952** Wilson, *Hemlock and After*	**1953** Coronation of Queen Elizabeth II; Edmund Hillary and Tenzing Norgay climb Mount Everest
1953 DNA structure discovered by Francis Crick and James Watson	**1953** Hartley, *The Go-Between*; Thomas, *Under Milk Wood*	**1954** Roger Bannister runs four-minute mile
	1954 Tolkien, *The Fellowship of the Ring*; Amis, *Lucky Jim*; Rattigan, *Separate Tables*; Golding, *Lord of the Flies*	**1955** Algerian uprising against French rule begins
1955 ITV launched	**1955** Larkin, *The Less Deceived*; Beckett, *Waiting for Godot*	**1956** Suez crisis: British and French troops withdraw from Suez canal zone; Hungarian anti-Soviet rebellion
	1956 Osborne, *Look Back in Anger*	
1957 Rock and Roll: Bill Haley arrives in UK Jodrell Bank space telescope inaugurated	**1957** Hughes, *The Hawk in the Rain*; Osborne, *The Entertainer*; Sillitoe, *Saturday Night and Sunday Morning*; Braine, *Room at the Top*	**1957** Malayan independence

1958 First hovercraft built; long-playing 33rpm records and stereo record players introduced; Campaign for Nuclear Disarmament formed;

1959 First British motorway, the M1, opens; Mini car invented

1960 Lady Chatterley trial; Royal Shakespeare Company formed; *Coronation Street* begins

1961 Yuri Gagarin is first man in space; Contraceptive pill available in Britain

1963 Beatlemania; first James Bond film, *Dr No*

1965 Mary Whitehouse launches 'Clean Up TV' campaign

1966 England wins the football World Cup

1967 Jet-boat racer Donald Campbell dies when Bluebird crashes; Marshall McLuhan: *The Medium is the Message;* first heart transplant operation

1968 Breathalyser tests introduced

1969 Concorde makes supersonic maiden flight; Woodstock festival; Isle of Wight festival stars Bob Dylan

1970 North Sea oil discovered; the Beatles split; *New English Bible* published; damages paid to parents of thalidomide babies

1958 Pinter, *The Birthday Party*; Murdoch, *The Bell*; Pym, *A Glass of Blessings*; Betjeman, *Collected Poems*; Achebe, *Things Fall Apart*

1959 Spark, *Memento Mori*; Wesker, *Roots*; MacInnes, *Absolute Beginners*

1960 Pinter, *The Caretaker*; Larkin, *The Whitsun Weddings*

1961 Spark, *The Prime of Miss Jean Brodie*

1962 Lessing, *The Golden Notebook*; Burgess, *A Clockwork Orange*; Alvarez, *The New Poetry*

1963 Amis, *One Fat Englishman*; Dunn, *Up the Junction*

1964 Larkin, *The Whitsun Weddings*

1965 Bond, *Saved;* Pinter, *The Homecoming*

1966 Heaney, *Death of a Naturalist*; Rhys, *Wide Sargasso Sea*; Scott, *The Jewel in the Crown*; Stoppard, *Rosencrantz and Guildenstern are Dead*

1967 Orton, *Loot*; O'Brien, *The Third Policeman*

1968 Stoppard, *The Real Inspector Hound*

1969 Fowles, *The French Lieutenant's Woman*; Orton, *What the Butler Saw*

1970 Hughes, *Crow*; Farrell, *Troubles*

1959 Fidel Castro comes to power in Cuba; Tibet invaded by China

1960 National Service abolished

1961 Berlin Wall constructed

1962 Cuban Missile Crisis; Nelson Mandela jailed

1963 Assassination of US president John F. Kennedy

1964 Death penalty for murder abolished

1965 First US offensive in Vietnam; death of Winston Churchill

1966 Cultural Revolution in China

1968 Assassination of Martin Luther King; Soviet invasion of Czechoslovakia; Riots in Paris

1969 British troops sent to Northern Ireland

8 3

1972 Pocket calculator using microchip technology invented by Clive Sinclair; John Betjeman made Poet Laureate; *Cosmopolitan* launched

1973 Capital Radio and LBC go on air

1976 National Theatre opens; Punk rock; Louise Brown, the world's first 'test-tube baby', born

1977 The Queen's Silver Jubilee

1979 Trevor Francis becomes first £1 million footballer

1982 Channel 4 launched; *Mary Rose* raised after 400 years

1983 Burrell collection opens in Glasgow

1984 Band Aid concert organised by Bob Geldof; Ted Hughes becomes Poet Laureate; Torvill and Dean win Olympic gold for ice-dancing; scientists warn of 'greenhouse effect'

1985 First CDs introduced

1971 Bond, *Lear*; Hill, *Mercian Hymns*

1972 Stoppard, *Jumpers*

1973 Murdoch, *The Black Prince*; Johnson, *Christie Malry's Own Double-Entry*; Farrell, *The Siege of Krishnapur*

1974 Larkin, *High Windows*; Stoppard, *Travesties*; Ayckbourn, *The Norman Conquests*

1975 Heaney, *North*; Pinter, *No Man's Land*, Griffiths, *Comedians*; Bradbury, *The History Man*

1977 Drabble, *The Ice Age*, Pym, *Quartet in Autumn*

1978 Murdoch, *The Sea, The Sea*; McEwan, *The Cement Garden*

1980 Friel, *Translations*; Golding, *Rites of Passage*

1981 Rushdie, *Midnight's Children*; Gray, *Lanark*

1982 Churchill, *Top Girls*; Boyd, *An Ice-Cream War*

1983 Swift, *Waterland*

1984 Carter, *Nights at the Circus*; Banks, *The Wasp Factory*; Amis, *Money*

1985 Ackroyd, *Hawksmoor;* Hare and Brenton, *Pravda;* Mo, *Sour Sweet*; Winterson, *Oranges Are Not The Only Fruit*

1987 Lochhead, *Mary Queen of Scots Got Her Head Chopped Off*; McEwan, *The Child in Time*

1971 Decimal currency introduced

1972 Bloody Sunday massacre in Northern Ireland

1973 Britain joins the EEC

1975 Margaret Thatcher becomes leader of Conservative Party

1976 Israeli raid on Entebbe

1979 Fall of Shah of Iran; Russia invades Afghanistan

1980 John Lennon shot; Rhodesia becomes Zimbabwe; Solidarity created in Poland; Ronald Reagan becomes US president

1981 Prince Charles marries Lady Diana Spencer; Toxteth and Brixton riots

1982 Falklands War

1984 IRA bomb Conservative Party at Brighton; miners' strike begins

1986 Chernobyl nuclear disaster

1988 Stephen Hawking: *A Brief History of Time*

1990 Space Shuttle Discovery places Hubble Telescope in Earth orbit

1991 Helen Sharman is first Briton to go into space; Freddie Mercury dies of Aids

1992 World Wide Web created, Internet takes off

1993 New Tate Gallery opens in St Ives; BSB satellite television launched

1994 Channel Tunnel opens; National Lottery begins

1996 Shakespeare's Globe Theatre opens

1997 Dolly the sheep is first mammal to be cloned; BSE ('mad cow disease') crisis

1998 *Fatwa* on Salman Rushdie lifted

1999 Millennium Dome built; Andrew Motion becomes Poet Laureate; concerns over genetically modified foods

2000 Tate Modern opens; Digital television begins

2002 The Queen's Golden Jubilee; *Punch* magazine closes after 160 years

1988 Rushdie, *The Satanic Verses*; Lodge, *Nice Work*

1989 Barnes, *A History of the World in 10½ Chapters*; Kelman, *A Disaffection;* Ishiguro, *Remains of the Day*

1990 Friel, *Dancing at Lughnasa*; Byatt, *Possession*; Amis, *London Fields*

1991 Carter, *Wise Children*; Barker, *Regeneration*

1992 Gray, *Poor Things;* Ondaatje, *The English Patient;* Hornby, *Fever Pitch*

1993 Doyle, *Paddy Clarke Ha Ha Ha*

1994 Kelman, *How Late It Was, How Late*; Atwood, *The Robber Bride*; Duffy, *Selected Poems;* de Bernières, *Captain Corelli's Mandolin*

1995 Atkinson, *Behind the Scenes at the Museum;* Barker, *Ghost Road*

1996 Swift, *Last Orders*

1997 Roy, *The God of Small Things;* Garner, *Strandloper*

1998 McEwan, *Amsterdam*

1999 Heaney, *Beowulf;* Coetzee, *Disgrace*

2000 Pullman, *The Amber Spyglass*; Tremain, *Music & Silence;* Smith, *White Teeth*

2001 McEwan, *Atonement;* Sage, *Bad Blood;* Atwood, *Blind Assassin*

1988 Lockerbie disaster

1989 Fall of the Berlin Wall

1990 Reunification of Germany

1991 Gulf War following Iraqi invasion of Kuwait; end of apartheid in South Africa; release of the Birmingham Six

1992 Serbia announces plan to create new Yugoslavian state

1993 Murder of Stephen Lawrence; murder of Jamie Bulger; IRA bombing campaign on mainland Britain

1996 Scott enquiry into arms to Iraq

1997 Death of Diana, Princess of Wales; election of Labour government under Tony Blair; Scotland votes for its own parliament, Wales votes for its own assembly

1998 Northern Ireland peace plan

1999 War with Serbia over ethnic cleansing of Kosovo

2000 Foot and mouth disease closes farms

2001 11 September terrorist attacks on America

2002 East Timor gains independence from Indonesia

GLOSSARY OF TERMS

Alliteration A formal element of poetry: the repetition of consonants at the beginning of words, used to achieve various effects including that of emphasis. Used to striking effect by Dylan Thomas in *Under Milk Wood*.

Absurd, Theatre of the a term used to characterise the work of a number of European and American dramatists of the 1950s and early 1960s, such as Samuel Beckett and Eugene Ionesco (1912-94) as well as Harold Pinter. In both content and form their plays are shaped by a view of life as being irrational and meaningless, with plots which deny any notion of logical or 'realistic' development.

Beat generation A group of anti-establishment American writers who emerged in the 1950s, including Jack Kerouac (1922-69), Allen Ginsberg (1926-97) and William Burroughs (1914-97). The word 'beat' – as in exhausted – was street language already used by jazz musicians, but these writers were also drawn to the term by its associations with rhythmic *beat* and with *beatitude*. Influenced by drugs, jazz, sex and Zen Buddhism, they set out to create a new kind of free-form literature, which would be spontaneous, unpretentious and anti-intellectual.

Black comedy Particularly in theatre, but also in films and novels, a form that makes comedy out of disturbing subjects like death, illness and war, and is not afraid to risk causing offence through unpredictability and a challenge to conventional notions of good taste. The plays of Joe Orton (see page 31) are a good example.

Campus novel A novel whose action is set within a university or college: usually comic in tone, and with a lecturer as central figure. An early example is Kingsley Amis's *Lucky Jim* (1954), but the campus novel became a sub-genre of its own in the 1970s, largely through the fictional work of high-profile academics such as Malcolm Bradbury, David Lodge and, in the United States, Alison Lurie.

Colonialism A system whereby distant settlements, or colonies, are controlled by a government in the home country. Authority may be exercised over the native population by the colonists, as well as over the colonists by the government at home; both kinds are likely, with the passing of time, to provoke an 'anti-colonialist' struggle.

Existentialism A philosophy with an emphasis on individual freedom, based on the belief that 'existence precedes essence', and a consequent rejection of the idea that there is a common humanity which determines a person's character or role in life. In literature it found expression in the 1940s and 1950s in the works of the French writers Jean-Paul Sartre (1905-80) and Albert Camus (1913-60), whose novels explore the idea of the hero as a character who is thrown into the world and has to confront the situation of being in charge of his personal destiny, without any external or 'objective' moral standards to guide him.

Genre A literary (or filmic) type or class, following certain conventions which help to create expectations and responses in the reader, and the audience. Examples include science fiction (in which a futuristic 'other world' setting is often used as a vehicle for ideas about the contemporary world), the Western, romance, crime fiction, fantasy fiction and horror. There are also many 'sub-genres' including the campus novel and 'chick-lit'. The term 'genre fiction' is sometimes used as a synonym for popular fiction, and used to distinguish it from 'literary' fiction, which is conventionally held to transcend genre writing.

Magic realism Fiction that presents fantastic or magical events as if they were ordinary, within an otherwise realistic plot and setting. Though there are precedents such as *Don Quixote*, this form became newly prominent and influential in the work of post-war South American novelists, notably *One Hundred Years of Solitude* (1967) by the Colombian writer Gabriel García Márquez. British writers Salman Rushdie and Angela Carter have adopted elements of magic realism in their work.

Modernism A tendency that responded to new currents in early 20th-century life and thought, particularly the changed pace of life, and new understandings of the workings of the mind via Darwin and Freud. Formally, it is characterised by experimentation – trying to find new forms to do justice to the revolutions in sensibility. In literature, formal experimentation meant a break with the more stable and traditional (realist) forms of expression in favour of fragmented stream-of-consciousness narratives, poetic images and the use of myth. Writers as different as James Joyce, T.S. Eliot and Virginia Woolf are regarded as modernist.

Nationalism Strong allegiance to the culture, and the material interests, of one's own nation. This can have different emphases in different circumstances: the nationalism of those defending their own language, territory or rights against hostile outside forces differs from the more aggressive forms of national self-assertion, as manifested in the racism of the 'British National Party'. The term is a difficult one to handle, since the different forms of nationalism are often confused, or overlap with one another.

Naturalism This term overlaps with realism (see page 88) but has a narrower application. It was originally applied to influential new movements in the literature and theatre of the later 19th century, whose leaders were the French novelist Emile Zola (1840-1902) and the Norwegian dramatist Henrik Ibsen (1828-1906). Both aimed to demonstrate that human lives are shaped by the forces of *nature* rather than by God, and more specifically by socio-economic factors that are beyond the control of the individual. From this perspective, naturalist writers dealt in a sober, often sombre way with the lives of ordinary people, avoiding extravagant plots. Naturalism has come to refer primarily to a style of accurate external representation in literature and the other arts.

Parody Imitation with a comic or satirical (see page 88) intention, intended to mock its original, sometimes affectionately, sometimes with malice. Parody typically attempts to copy aspects of its target very closely, and the good parody may even be so close to its target that it is not recognised by all as a parody; or it may survive in its own right after the parodied item has been forgotten, as happens here and there in Lewis Carroll's *Alice* books.

Picaresque From the Spanish word *picaro*, a rogue. The form of novel described as 'picaresque' first appeared in 16th-century Spain, typically portraying an ingenious trickster living off his wits while travelling through a variety of low-life settings. The term was later applied to 18th-century novels which describe the episodic adventures of a lively and resourceful hero on a journey, such as *Tom Jones* by Henry Fielding and *Moll Flanders* by Daniel Defoe. A good example of the modern 'picaresque' novel is *Hurry On Down* (1953) by John Wain, often linked to the 'angry young man' movement, and the term continues to be found useful, being applied to works as diverse as the film *Forrest Gump* (1994) and the novels of the New York writer Paul Auster (1947-).

Post-colonial literature Description of writing coming from, or dealing with, the peoples and cultures of lands which were formerly European colonies (often part of the British Empire) such as Africa, the West Indies and India, and which emerged from colonial rule after the end of World War II. Most post-colonial writers have chosen to write in English, the language of their former colonisers, although some, such as West Indian writers Derek Walcott and V.S. Naipaul, have switched in and out of local Creole and standard English to emphasise the hybrid nature of the post-colonial world. Other examples are the Nigerian writer Chinua Achebe (1930-) and Indian writers Arundhati Roy (1961-) and Vikram Seth (1952-).

Post-modernism As the word implies, post-modernism is essentially an extension of, but also a reaction against, pre-World War II modernism, taking further its key characteristics of innovation, experimentation and self-awareness; it responds to developments in communication that have increasingly broken down barriers of space and time, making a variety of past and present materials instantly available to us. Post-modernist literature reflects this in its fragmentation, its lack of conventional coherence, and its delight in mixing elements of popular and high culture. While some authors, such as Angela Carter or the experimental novelist and film-maker B.S. Johnson (1933-73), can be labelled as post-modernist, the word also refers to a common element in more mainstream modern writing; in their ironic play with conventions and with different levels of narrative, the novels of writers like Martin Amis can be said to demonstrate a post-modernist sensibility.

Realism Ever since Plato, philosophers have disagreed over the nature of the 'real', so it is not surprising that realism is a difficult term to pin down; it can refer to surface realism, or to an 'inner' realism which may be in conflict with it. The so-called 'classic realist text', as in the work of 19th-century novelists such as Tolstoy, Balzac and George Eliot, aims to combine the two levels, by capturing the essential forces and conflicts in society through a convincing depiction of representative environments, events and characters. Many novels, films and plays still follow this common-sense tradition, while being challenged by rival versions of realism, or of anti-realism. Realism is perhaps best seen as a fluid set of conventions, designed to create an impression of real life, however that may be defined.

Regional novel A novel set in a real and well-defined locality, with which the reader is not usually expected to be familiar. The Brontës could be described as early 'regional novelists', with their descriptions of rural Yorkshire locations. The industrial or urban regional novel emerged with writers such as Dickens and George Eliot in the 19th century. The genre flourished in the 1950s in novels such as John Braine's *Room at the Top* (1957), set in a Yorkshire town, and Alan Sillitoe's *Saturday Night and Sunday Morning* (1958), set in Nottingham.

Satire A mode of writing that combines criticism with comic ridicule. Often light and witty, it is also undertaken with a serious purpose – to expose hypocrisy and attack corruption and stupidity. Satire may use parody and irony as tools. In post-war literature, satire flourished in the works of Angus Wilson (1913-91), Evelyn Waugh and Kingsley Amis, among others. In the 1960s satire became more widely fashionable through, for instance, the theatrical revue *Beyond the Fringe*, by Peter Cook, Dudley Moore, Alan Bennett and Jonathan Miller, and the weekly BBC TV programme *That Was the Week That Was.*

Social realism A form of realism (see above) that puts particular emphasis on the objective depiction of people living in a specific environment within society, described in unsparing detail. The vivid descriptive power of the camera means that the most striking post-war examples have been in film and television rather than in literature, for instance in the work of Mike Leigh and of Ken Loach: good examples of British social realism are Loach's *Cathy Come Home* (1965) and *Kes* (1969).

Totalitarianism An anti-democratic form of government in which the ruler is an absolute dictator, without being restricted by constitution, laws or opposition. Both Fascism and Communism, as they developed in the 20th century, are forms of totalitarianism.

Well-made play A conventionally structured drama which involves the audience in the experiences of believable characters, and creates problems and tensions which are then neatly resolved. This form of naturalist drama dominated the English stage for much of the 20th century through the work of writers like John Galsworthy, Somerset Maugham, Noel Coward and subsequently Terence Rattigan; it, and the audience who support it, have met increasingly outspoken opposition from those who find it predictable and conservative, even when dealing with apparently bold themes.

BIOGRAPHICAL GLOSSARY

Kingsley Amis (1922-95), novelist and poet. Born in south London and educated at St John's College, Oxford. He did army service, and taught English for 12 years at the universities of Swansea and Cambridge before deciding to become a full-time writer. His time in Wales was reflected in several novels, notably *The Old Devils*, for which he won the Booker Prize in 1986. His first popular success was *Lucky Jim*, published in 1954. Originally placed among the 'angry young men', he adopted an increasingly reactionary public persona as he grew older and some of his later novels, such as *Stanley and the Women* (1984) were seen by some commentators as misogynistic.

Martin Amis (1949-), novelist. Son of Kingsley Amis. He was expelled from several schools in Britain, Spain and America, but got a first-class degree in English literature at Oxford. He was a literary critic for several newspapers and the literary editor of the *New Statesman* in the late 1970s. His reputation as a writer was established after the publication of his first novel, *The Rachel Papers*, when he was 24, and furthered with *Dead Babies* (1975) and *Success* (1978). Much of his writing, for example *Night Train* (1997), has been influenced by American fiction, particularly that of Vladimir Nabokov and Saul Bellow.

Margaret Atwood (1939-) novelist, poet and critic. She was born in Ottawa, Canada and spent much of her childhood in the northern Ontario and Quebec bush country. She started writing at the age of five but didn't start school full-time until the age of 11. After graduating from Toronto University she did a variety of jobs before turning to full-time writing. Her first volume of poetry, *The Circle Game*, was published in 1966. She has now written more than 30 books of fiction, poetry and critical essays, and gained an international reputation, particularly for feminist novels such as *Lady Oracle* (1976) and *The Robber Bride* (1994). She has won many literary awards and honours, including the Booker Prize for her tenth novel, *The Blind Assassin* (2000).

John Betjeman (1906-84), poet. Born in Highgate, north London, he was educated at public school and Oxford, where he became friendly with the poets W.H. Auden and Louis MacNeice. He left without a degree and was a schoolmaster for a short time. His first collection of poems, *Mount Zion*, was published in 1931 and was followed by many other collections including *A Few Late Chrysanthemums* (1954) and the extremely successful *Collected Poems* (1958, expanded in 1962). He was also interested in architecture, and wrote various works on the subject as well as editing and writing a series of *Shell Guides to Britain*, some of which were illustrated by his friend, the artist John Piper. He was appointed Poet Laureate in 1972.

Edward Bond (1934-) playwright. He was born in Holloway, north London, and left school when he was 15. During the blitz in 1940 he was evacuated to Cornwall and later to East Anglia, an area which provides the setting for several of his plays including *The Fool* (1975), about the poet John Clare. After school he worked in factories and offices, and did his national service from 1953 to 1955. He has said he considers his lack of formal education to be an advantage for a playwright. Inspired by a production of *Macbeth* he saw while at school, he began to write plays, many of which went unpublished. He joined the Writer's Group of the English Stage Company at the Royal Court in 1958. They premiered *Saved* in 1965, but when Bond refused to make the cuts demanded by the Lord Chamberlain it was banned. As well as many plays for theatre, such as *War Plays* (1985) about life after a nuclear holocaust, he has written film and television screenplays, including *Walkabout* (1971), directed by Nicolas Roeg.

Angela Carter (1940-92), novelist, poet and essayist: the leading exponent of British magic realism (see Glossary of Terms). She was born in Eastbourne but went to live with her grandmother in Yorkshire during the blitz in World War II. In an act of rebellion against her over-possessive mother she did badly at A-levels and, after school, became a reporter on the Croydon Advertiser. She married an industrial chemist and moved to Bristol, but became bored with being a housewife and enrolled at Bristol University, where she read English. She wrote her first novel, *Shadow Dance* (1966) in her second year. Later she taught creative writing at several British universities, including the University of East Anglia, as well as in Japan and the USA. As well as writing fiction she translated the fairy stories of Charles Perrault, and published three collections of short stories including *The Bloody Chamber* (1979). Her journalism appeared in almost every major British publication. Together with Neil Jordan, she wrote the film script of her story 'The Company of Wolves', and she also adapted her second novel, *The Magic Toyshop*, for film. By the time of her death from cancer at the age of 51 she had become one of Britain's most influential and widely studied writers.

Caryl Churchill (1938-) playwright. Born in London and educated in Montreal and in England.

Her first play, *Downstairs*, (1958) was performed by a student dramatic society when she was an undergraduate at Oxford. She married soon after leaving university and had three sons, and during the 1960s mainly wrote radio drama. In 1972 she was commissioned to write for the Royal Court Theatre, for whom she wrote *Owners* and many subsequent plays which were radical and feminist in tone. Much of her work, including *Light Shining in Buckinghamshire* and *Cloud Nine,* resulted from improvisational workshops conducted with the Joint Stock Theatre Group. Later plays include *Mad Forest* (1990) and *The Striker* (1994), and she has also written several television plays.

Carol Ann Duffy (1955-), poet and playwright. She was born in Glasgow but moved to Stafford when she was six. Her first poetry collection, *Fleshweathercock* (1973) was published while she was still at school. She studied philosophy at Liverpool University and in order to be near her boyfriend, the poet Adrian Henri, stayed on in the city where she made her reputation as a playwright in the early 1980s with *Take My Husband* and *Cavern of Dreams*, both produced at the Liverpool Playhouse. Her reputation as a poet grew steadily and her 1993 collection, *Mean Time*, won the Whitbread Poetry Award. She has now published five collections of poetry and has won many awards and fellowships.

William Golding (1911-93), poet and novelist. He was born in Cornwall and educated at Marlborough Grammar School and at Oxford. After university he worked as an actor and writer, and then became a schoolmaster. He served in the Royal Navy in World War II and returned to teaching after the war. His first published volume was a collection of poems (*Poems*, 1935), but his first novel, *The Lord of the Flies*, was not published until 1954, after being rejected by 21 publishers. His next novel, *The Inheritors*, was published in 1955. Subsequent works include *Pincher Martin* (1956), *Free Fall* (1959) and *The Spire* (1964). He won the Booker Prize in 1980 for *Rites of Passage*, and was awarded the Nobel Prize for literature in 1983. His last two books, *Close Quarters* (1987) and *Fire Down Below* (1989), completed the trilogy begun with *Rites of Passage*: all three novels portray life aboard a ship during the Napoleonic Wars.

Seamus Heaney (1939-), poet. He grew up on the family farm in County Derry, Northern Ireland and trained as a secondary school teacher after leaving St Columb's College in Derry. He later became a lecturer at Queen's University in Belfast. He came to critical attention with his first collection of poems, *Death of a Naturalist*, in 1968. In 1972 he moved to the Republic of Ireland, living first in County Wicklow and then in Dublin. In the 1980s he began to spend frequent periods at American universities as a visiting professor, and between 1989 and 1994 he was Professor of Poetry at Oxford. Other collections include *The Haw Lantern* (1987) and *New Selected Poems 1966-87* (1990). In 1995 he was awarded the Nobel prize for his international contribution to literature and his very successful translation of *Beowulf* was published in 1999.

Ted Hughes (1930-98), poet. He was born in Mytholmroyd in West Yorkshire, and the craggy landscape and harsh dialect of his childhood, together with his father's memories of the violence of World War I, informed the poetry he began writing in his teens. After leaving grammar school he did two years' national service with the RAF. He switched from studying English to archaeology and anthropology at Cambridge, where he met Sylvia Plath; they married in 1956. They went to live in America where he taught English and creative writing at the University of Massachusetts. Plath helped to get his first collection, *The Hawk in the Rain*, published in 1957, which established his reputation as one of the most important poets of the post-war period. Plath and Hughes returned to England in 1959 and in 1963 she committed suicide, shortly after the publication of her novel *The Bell Jar*. Hughes later took legal action to prevent the production of a film about his and Plath's life together. His poetry during the 1970s, such as *Crow* (1970) was dark and turbulent; much of it also shows a concern with mythology. He also wrote several books of children's verse, notably *The Iron Man*. In 1984 he was appointed Poet Laureate, and his Laureate poems are gathered in *Rain-Charm for the Duchy* (1992).

Philip Larkin (1922-85), poet and novelist. The son of a local government official, he grew up in Coventry. He went to Oxford University where he got to know other writers including Kingsley Amis. After leaving Oxford in 1943 he worked in various libraries before becoming librarian in 1955 at the University of Hull, a post he held until his death. *The Less Deceived* (1955) was the collection of poems that first attracted widespread attention, and *The Whitsun Weddings* (1964) and *High Windows* (1974) consolidated his reputation as perhaps the most significant English poet since the war. He also wrote two novels in the 1940s, *Jill* and *A Girl in Winter*, while his lifelong love of jazz was celebrated in the collection *All What Jazz*. He never married, and lived in a series of drab rented rooms and flats before buying a house in Hull in 1974, which he shared with his companion Monica Jones. He kept voluminous diaries which, on his instructions, were destroyed on his death but there was still enough material for an extensive biography by one of his literary executors, Andrew Motion (*Philip Larkin: A Writer's Life*, 1993). Although the book did not tarnish his reputation as a poet, some readers were shocked by revelations of his casual racism and other 'politically incorrect' attitudes and habits.

Doris Lessing (1919-), novelist and playwright. Born in Iran, she grew up on a farm in Southern Rhodesia where she spent a lonely childhood. She left her Catholic convent school at 14 and immersed herself in reading and writing fiction. In the early 1940s she joined the Communist Party, and this period of her life is reflected in the autobiographical novel *A Ripple from the Storm*, (1965) one of her five-volume *Children of Violence* sequence. In 1950 she moved to London where her novel *The Grass Is Singing* – the story of a white South African farmer's wife and her black houseboy who is charged with his employer's murder – was published to great acclaim. Her best-known novel is *The Golden Notebook*, (1962) which was hailed as the most sophisticated of all the 'women's liberation' works of the 1960s. She is known as a challenging and formally experimental writer whose work reflects a wide range of interests, including science fiction.

Liz Lochhead (1947-), poet, playwright, performance artist. She was born in Motherwell, Scotland and after school trained as a painter at Glasgow School of Art, where she also began writing poems. Her first collection, *Memo for Spring*, was published in 1972. She taught art for several years in Glasgow and Bristol, until winning a writing fellowship in 1978 enabled her to become a full-time writer. In the same year her revue *Sugar and Spice* was performed. In the early 1980s she began writing plays inspired by literature and history, such as *Blood and Ice* (1982), based on the life of Mary Shelley, and *Mary Queen of Scots Got Her Head Chopped Off* (1987). She travels a great deal performing her work, which includes songs, sketches and monologues (some of which were collected in *True Confessions and New Clichés,* 1985).

Ian McEwan (1948-), novelist. Born in Aldershot, Hampshire, the army town where his father was a sergeant-major, he travelled widely with his family during his childhood. After reading English at Sussex University he became the first student on the postgraduate creative writing course at the University of East Anglia, which had been set up by Malcolm Bradbury. Freelance work for the *Radio Times* helped finance his early writing. He came to fame with his first published book, a collection of short stories entitled *First Love, Last Rites* (1975), and *The Cement Garden* (1978) reinforced his reputation as a powerful teller of disturbing and

anarchic stories. *The Comfort of Strangers* (1981) was adapted for cinema by Harold Pinter. His 1987 novel, *The Child in Time*, won a Whitbread award, and *Amsterdam* (1998) won the Booker prize. His other work has included several screenplays including *The Ploughman's Lunch* (1993), television plays and an oratorio on an anti-nuclear theme.

Iris Murdoch (1919-99), novelist and philosopher. She was born in Dublin of Anglo-Irish parents but grew up in west London. After graduating from Somerville College, Oxford, she became a civil servant and then worked for the United Nations Relief Organisation in London and abroad. During this period she met several influential philosophers including Jean-Paul Sartre, who helped fuel her interest in existentialism, and she went back to Oxford to study philosophy under Ludwig Wittgenstein. In 1948 she became a fellow and tutor in philosophy at Oxford, and remained there until 1963, after which she earned her living as a writer. She married the literary critic John Bayley in 1956. Her first novel, *Under the Net*, was published in 1954, and during a prolific and very successful career she published over 25 novels, including the Booker prize-winning *The Sea, The Sea* (1978). She also wrote several works on philosophy and philosophers. In the late 1990s she was diagnosed with Alzheimer's disease, and the devastating effect of this illness on her life was documented by her husband in two volumes of autobiography, filmed as *Iris* in 2001.

Joe Orton (1933-67), playwright. Born into a working-class family in Leicester, he left school at 16 to train as an actor. When he was 18 he got a grant to go to RADA (Royal Academy of Dramatic Art) in London, where he met Kenneth Halliwell, who became his lover. They started writing plays together, but *Entertaining Mr Sloane* (1964) was published under Orton's name only and established his reputation for outrageous and anarchic black comedy. Halliwell became increasingly depressed and jealous after the success of *Loot* (1965); the couple's relationship was also undermined by Orton's promiscuity, the details of which he recorded in his diaries. In 1967 Halliwell beat Orton to death with a hammer, and then committed suicide. Orton's last play, *What the Butler Saw*, was produced posthumously at the Royal Court in 1967, to mixed reviews, but his fame has been secured by regular revivals of his work, and by John Lahr's biography *Prick Up Your Ears*, filmed in 1987 by Stephen Frears from a script by Alan Bennett.

John Osborne (1929-94), playwright. He was born in the London suburb of Fulham and after leaving school became, briefly, a journalist and then an actor. He began to write plays during the years he spent touring with a repertory company, the first of which was performed in 1950. He made his name as the original 'angry young man' with *Look Back in Anger* in 1956 (see page 19). Osborne always expressed his anger against contemporary society in his work as well as in the many letters he wrote to the press. He continued writing plays throughout the 1960s and '70s, including *Inadmissible Evidence* (1964) and *A Sense of Detachment* (1972), but these were not as well-received critically as his early work. He also wrote several film scripts, including the successful *Tom Jones* (1963), and two volumes of autobiography, the second of which was called *Damn You, England* (1994).

George Orwell (pen-name of Eric Blair, 1903-50), novelist, journalist. Born in India, he was brought to England as a child and educated at Eton. From 1922 to 1928 he served in Burma with the Indian Imperial Police, and his experiences were reflected in his first novel, *Burmese Days* (1934). Rejecting his colonial background, he resigned and for the next two years lived in poverty in Paris, and then returned to England where he worked as a school teacher and in a bookshop, a period recorded in *Down and Out in Paris and London* (1933). He continued to publish both fiction and non-fiction; in 1936 a commission to write about the lives of working-class people in the north of England led to *The Road to Wigan Pier*, after which he went to Spain to fight for the Republicans during the civil war, and was wounded. (*See Homage to Catalonia*, 1938). During World War II he was a member of the Home Guard, and worked prolifically as a journalist and as an overseas broadcaster for BBC radio. His name became widely known with the publication of *Animal Farm* in 1945, which, with *Nineteen Eighty-Four* (1949), remains his most popular work.

Harold Pinter (1930-) playwright. The son of a Jewish tailor, he was born in east London and went to Hackney Downs Grammar School. His first poetry was published in periodicals before he was 20. In 1949 he was fined by magistrates for refusing to do national service because he was a conscientious objector. He became an actor and wrote his first play, *The Room* (1957) while on tour with a repertory company. His next play, *The Birthday Party* (1958), received mainly hostile reviews (although Noel Coward was a fan), but his distinctive voice was soon recognised and most of his subsequent plays – which include *The Caretaker* (1963), *The Homecoming* (1965) and *No Man's Land* (1975) – were critically and commercially successful. The term 'Pinteresque' was coined to describe his style of writing, particularly the faltering, pause-ridden dialogue

used by his characters. Pinter has also written widely for radio, television and, especially, cinema: for the exiled Hollywood director Joseph Losey he wrote *The Servant* (1964), *Accident* (1967), *The Go-Between* (1970) and an adaptation of Proust's *Remembrance of Times Past* which was published but never filmed.

Philip Pullman (1946-), novelist. Born in Norwich, he travelled the world as a child because his father was in the RAF. He read English at Oxford, and wrote his first novel, for adults, while he was doing a postgraduate teaching course. By this time he was married and had a child, and although he wanted to concentrate on writing he got a job teaching in a middle school in order to support his family. His second book, a science fiction/fantasy novel, *Galatea* (1977) was also for adults. He began writing for children when he found that there were very few plays suitable for his students to perform; *Ruby in the Smoke*, *Count Karlstein* and *The Firework Maker's Daughter*, which he later rewrote as novels, all began as plays. After several years in schools, he became a lecturer in adult and children's literature at Westminster College in Oxford. After the publication of *Northern Lights* in 1995 he gave up teaching. He writes in a shed in his back garden, using a ballpoint pen and paper.

Barbara Pym (1913-80), novelist. The daughter of a Shropshire solicitor, she was educated at St Hilda's College, Oxford. She served in the WRNS during World War II, and later worked as an editorial secretary at the International African Institute in London. Her novels, which include *Excellent Women* (1952) and *A Glass of Blessings* (1958), are satirical and tragi-comic portrayals of, typically, middle-class, churchgoing spinsters in a milieu she herself understood very well. In the 1960s her writing became unfashionable and she found it impossible to get work published, but in 1977 she was 'rediscovered' after both Philip Larkin and Lord David Cecil chose her as one of the most underrated novelists of the century. This stimulated renewed interest in her work and encouraged her to start writing again, resulting in *Quartet in Autumn* (1977) and *The Sweet Dove Died* (1978).

Jean Rhys (?1890-1975), novelist. Born in Dominica to a Creole mother and Welsh father, she came to England in 1907 and trained at the Royal Academy of Dramatic Art. Needing to earn money after her father's death, she worked as a chorus girl and a film extra, and as a cook during World War I. She began to write in Paris, where much of her early work, such as *The Left Bank,* 1927, is set. After the publication of *Good Morning, Midnight* (1939), the story of a lonely middle-aged woman adrift in Paris, Rhys was forgotten as a writer. She returned to England and lived in poverty in Devon for almost 20 years, until a BBC producer discovered her whereabouts and she was encouraged to start writing again. *Wide Sargasso Sea* was published in 1966 to great critical acclaim, and Rhys became a cult writer.

Salman Rushdie (1947-), novelist. Born in Bombay to a Muslim family and educated at public school and at King's College, Cambridge. He worked for a time in television in Pakistan, as an actor in London, and as an advertising copywriter. His first book, *Grimus*, was published in 1975, but he came to literary prominence with *Midnight's Children* in 1981, which was followed by a novel about Pakistan, *Shame* (1983). *The Satanic Verses* (1988) brought him notoriety after the Ayatollah Khomeini invoked a *fatwa* on him. He lived in hiding under police protection for several years. In the late 1990s he began to appear in public again at literary events and since then has become a member of the so-called 'glitterati'.

Tom Stoppard (1937-) playwright. Born Tomas Straussler in Zlin, Czechoslovakia, he moved with his family to Singapore when he was two years old. His father was killed there, and after the war the family moved to England, where he took the name of his English stepfather, a British army officer. After leaving school in Bristol he worked as a journalist on local newspapers, specialising in film and theatre criticism. He began writing plays; the first to attract major critical attention after it was performed by the National Theatre Company was *Rosencrantz and Guildenstern are Dead* (1966). This was followed by many other plays for theatre (of which *Jumpers*, 1972 and *Travesties*, 1974 are among the best known), as well as work for television and cinema. By 1977 he had become concerned with human rights issues, in particular with the situation of political dissidents in Eastern Europe, and became involved in campaigns including Amnesty International. *Every Good Boy Deserves Favour* (1977) is about a political dissident confined to a Soviet mental hospital. Subsequent major stage plays include *The Real Thing* (1982) and *Arcadia* (1993).

Dylan Thomas (1914-53), poet. He was born in Swansea, the son of the English master at Swansea Grammar School which he himself attended. He began to write poetry while still at school and worked as a journalist before moving to London in 1934, where he soon acquired a reputation for his flamboyant, hard-drinking lifestyle as much as for his exuberant poetry. His first book, *18 Poems*, was published as the result of a prize when he was only 19. He married Caitlin Macnamara in 1937, and they lived in great poverty with their three children, settling permanently in Laugharne in Wales in 1949. Rejected for military service in World War II, he worked instead with a documentary film unit, scripting many widely seen propaganda films. He also published many short stories, and broadcast frequently for BBC radio. His unique style of writing gradually won him a large following, particularly after the publication of *Deaths and Entrances* in 1946, which contains some of his best-known work. In 1949 he began making lecture tours to the USA, and died in New York – apparently as a result of alcoholic poisoning – shortly after a reading of what was to become his most famous single work, *Under Milk Wood*, in 1953.

Evelyn Waugh (1903-66), novelist. Born into an comfortable middle-class family in Hampstead, he was educated at public school, where he was bullied, and read modern history at Oxford. His father was a publisher and his brother, Alec Waugh, was a popular novelist. At Oxford he was a keen socialite and neglected his studies, graduating with a third-class degree. He went to art school and then worked for a short time as a schoolmaster, which provided material for his first novel, *Decline and Fall* (1928). Its success meant he was able to devote himself to writing full-time, and other novels which captured the manners and morals of upper-class life in the inter-war years followed, including *Vile Bodies* (1930) and *Scoop* (1938). During World War II he served in the Army, and his wartime experiences provided material for his *Sword of Honour* trilogy (*Men at Arms*, 1952; *Officers and Gentlemen*, 1955; *Unconditional Surrender*, 1961). His most popular work was *Brideshead Revisited*, published in 1945. He also wrote biographies and a volume of autobiography (*A Little Learning*, 1964).

Jeanette Winterson (1959-), novelist. Born in Manchester, she was raised to be a missionary by the evangelical family who adopted her, and was writing sermons by the age of eight. She learnt to read from the Bible, which was one of only six books her parents possessed. After leaving school she studied English at St Catherine's College, Oxford. Before becoming a full-time writer and publisher she worked as an assistant in a mental hospital and as a make-up artist in a funeral parlour. She drew on her own upbringing as well as on her lesbian identity in her first novel, *Oranges Are Not the Only Fruit* (1985), which won a Whitbread award, and was given a high-profile TV adaptation. She began experimenting with narrative style in her subsequent feminist novels, which include *Sexing the Cherry* (1989) and the controversial *Art and Lies* (1994).

FURTHER READING

POST-WAR LITERATURE, CULTURE AND SOCIETY

Arthur Marwick: *British Society Since 1945* (London 1982, revised edn 1996). Clear and informative survey and analysis of high and popular culture, and the diversity of social developments in Britain from 1945 to the 1990s.

Christopher Booker: *The Neophiliacs: the revolution in English life in the fifties and sixties* (London 1969). Classic account of the rise of the 'cultural revolution' in Britain, starting with the impact of rock 'n' roll in 1956.

Clive Bloom and Gary Day (eds): *Literature and Culture in Modern Britain*, Volume Two 1930-1955 and Volume Three 1956-1999 (London 2000). Part of a recent series about different aspects of British culture, including music, cinema and newspapers as well as literature and art.

Patricia Waugh: *Harvest of the Sixties: English literature and its background 1960 to 1990* (Oxford 1995).

Martin Stephen: *English Literature: a student guide* (London 2000). Basic guide, aimed at A-level students, including some material on post-war authors and texts.

Alan Sinfield (ed): *The Context of English Literature: Society and Literature 1945-1970* (London 1983). Collection of essays by lecturers from the University of Sussex.

THE NOVEL

Alan Massie: *The Novel Today; a critical guide to the British novel 1970-1989* (London 1993). Short introduction to many of the major post-war novelists and genres.

Malcolm Bradbury (ed): *The Novel Today: Contemporary Writers on Modern Fiction* (Glasgow, revised edn 1990). Collection of essays by novelists writing about their own, and others', fiction. Useful for students of modernism and post-modernism.

Lorna Sage: *Moments of Truth: twelve twentieth-century women writers* (London 2001). Collection of this highly respected writer and critic's essays and journalism on other writers including Iris Murdoch, Angela Carter and Jean Rhys.

DRAMA AND POETRY

Michelene Wandor: *Drama Today: a critical guide to British drama 1970-1990* (London 1993). Concise, straightforward guide to key themes, writers and plays.

Jonathan Bignell, Stephen Lacey and Madeleine Macmurrough-Kavanagh (eds): *British Television Drama Past, Present and Future* (Basingstoke 2000) Collection of essays by media professionals and academics, including contributions by writers Andrew Davies, John McGrath and Alan Plater.

Peter Childs: *The Twentieth Century in Poetry* (London 1999). An up-to-date critical survey of British poetry examined through the events of the 20th century. Includes chapters on poetry after the war, recent anthologies by male and female poets, Northern Irish and black British poets.

Aileen Christianson and Alison Lumsden (eds): *Contemporary Scottish Women Writers* (Edinburgh, 2000). Chapters on Liz Lochhead and Carol Ann Duffy.

GENERAL

Kenneth O. Morgan: *Twentieth-century Britain, a very short introduction* (Oxford 2000).

Margaret Drabble (ed): *The Oxford Companion to English Literature* (Oxford 1995). Regularly updated reference book with entries on individual writers as well as literary movements.

Frances Spalding: *British Art since 1900* (London, 1986).

Robert Murphy (ed): *The British Cinema Book* (London, second ed 2001). Interesting collection of essays on British cinema history, mostly post-World War II.

Britain's Century, year by year from 1900 to 2000. One of a series of illustrated reference books published by Dorling Kindersley, with entries on key events and historical landmarks written in the style of a contemporary newspaper.

WEBSITES

Two of the most useful sites with information and links about contemporary English fiction, drama and poetry are those belonging to *The Guardian* newspaper and the BBC:
www.books.guardian.co.uk/authors
www.bbc.co.uk/arts/books/

INDEX